Blueprints for Life

The Making of Great Men in the Bible

"All scripture is given by inspiration of God, and is profitable for doctrine, for reproof, for correction, for instruction in righteousness: That the man of God may be perfect, throughly furnished unto all good works."

(2 Timothy 3:16-17)

ISBN: 978-0-615-19566-7

All Scripture quotations are from the King James Bible 1611.

Visit our website at:
www.domelleministries.com

For more copies write to:
Allen Domelle Ministries
PO Box 19
Inwood, WV 25428
or call (304) 839-9531.

Table of Contents

FOREWORD

When I was a boy, we lived in Pueblo, Colorado, for a few years as my dad started and pastored a church in this city. I remember one morning, it had snowed the night before, and as the usual case was on a Sunday morning, I went to church with my dad to help prepare for the morning service. When we arrived at the church, my dad came over to my side of the car and opened the door to help me get into the church as the snow was deep. As my dad walked to the door of the church, I put my little feet into my dad's footprints and followed him all the way to the church door. When I remember this story in my life about putting my feet into my dad's footprints and following where he walked; I realize that we can become successful in life by simply following the footsteps of those who have walked before and make those footsteps a blueprint for our life.

This book that you are about to read is a study that I did on thirteen great men of the Bible. My hope is, that as you study this book, you will take the characteristics that have made these men into the men that they are and use them as a blueprint to follow in your life. My belief is if we will follow in their footsteps and make the characteristics that made these men great Christians a blueprint for our lives, we can be as successful as these men were and even do greater things for God.

Without a blueprint to follow in life, we are sure to fail. God has given us a blueprint to build our lives upon, and this blueprint is the Word of God. Let us take the examples that God has given us in His Word to learn from and use them so we can further the cause of Christ and avoid the mistakes that these men made. We can use these lessons to build upon the successes that these men achieved.

1

Having the Face of God

Deuteronomy 34:5-6, "So Moses the servant of the LORD died there in the land of Moab, according to the word of the LORD. And he buried him in a valley in the land of Moab, over against Beth-peor: but no man knoweth of his sepulchre unto this day."

Maybe no better compliment could Moses receive than to have God Himself think that no man was worthy to bury him. As we look in our text verse, we see that God thought to Himself that, because Moses was so close to Him, no man was worthy of holding Moses' funeral or burial. God decided to be the One who would hold the funeral and graveside service for Moses. What an honor! I mean, I would hope someday that God could look down from Heaven and see the life of Allen Domelle, and God would say to the preacher that is scheduled to hold my funeral, "Step aside; no man is worthy to hold this funeral service, so I will." That would be quite the honor for God to do this. The whole reason why God did this was because of the man who Moses was and how close Moses became to God in his lifetime. Let me explain by telling you the story of Moses' life.

Moses was born in the land of Egypt under the rule of a wicked Pharaoh who had forgotten all of the works that Joseph had done for this land. Pharaoh saw the Israelite people growing and becoming stronger and more in number than the Egyptians; therefore, Pharaoh decided to enact a law that would have every male who was born killed. This was the first time in history that we see abortion being made a law. The midwives of the land knew that this was wrong. By keeping the men children alive, they realized that obeying

God was more important than obeying laws that were in direct contradiction to the laws of God.

The mother of Moses was pregnant with him and delivered him during this time of history in Egypt. Instead of having him killed, she decided to put him in a basket and hide him in the bulrushes in the river. She told her daughter to keep an eye on him to see what would become of her son. As it would happen, the daughter of Pharaoh came to bathe in the very river in which Moses was placed. Hearing him cry, her heart went out to him and she took him to be her own son. As she held this baby, Moses' sister came over to see if she could help, and Pharaoh's daughter asked her to find someone to nurse and care for the child; and so it was that Moses' mother was able to nurse him and rear him as he became the son of Pharaoh's daughter.

Time had now passed and Moses became a grown man. Knowing that he was a Jew, he decided to identify with his own people instead of with Pharaoh and the Egyptians. Seeing an Egyptian smiting a Jewish man, Moses took matters into his own hands and killed the Egyptian which ended up causing him to run for his life and live in the wilderness for forty years.

We know the story of how Moses came back and became the leader of the Israelites to help deliver them from Egypt and take them to the Promised Land. Through his leadership, God used him to help deliver Israel from Egypt by sending the ten plagues; he led them through the Red Sea, and for forty years led these millions of people through the wilderness. Yet as we come to the end of his life, God saw fit to bury him, for no man was worthy to bury this great man of God.

Certainly Moses was a great man of God and there can be no argument to this fact. Probably no man of God in history had seen God perform more miracles through his ministry than Moses had seen. Yes, he was a great man of God and is a man who is worthy of studying his life and learning some of the characteristics that made him such a great man.

Let me give you some of the characteristics from the life of Moses that I believe made him the great man of God that he was. We can take these same characteristics and apply them to our lives. What was it that made him the man that he was?

1. He chose God's way over position and wealth.

Exodus 2:11, "And it came to pass in those days, when Moses was grown, that he went out unto his brethren, and looked on their burdens: and he spied an Egyptian smiting an Hebrew, one of his brethren."

Hebrews 11:24-25, "By faith Moses, when he was come to years, refused to be called the son of Pharaoh's daughter; Choosing rather to suffer affliction with the people of God, than to enjoy the pleasures of sin for a season;"

The truth is that Moses chose God's way over position and wealth. Moses could have inherited the riches of Pharaoh because he was an heir by being the adopted child of Pharaoh's daughter. He could have had a high position in the nation of Egypt if he would have just decided to keep quiet about who he was and who his people were. However, Moses realized that God's way was more important than having any position and having a substantial amount of wealth. We as Christians must learn this important truth and apply it to our lives.

There is no position and there is no amount of wealth that should be able to lure us away from doing what God commands us to do. If we ever have to choose between serving God and having position and wealth, we should always choose what God commands and not position or wealth. Position and wealth may give you pleasure for a season, but eventually that season will end and when it ends,

8

if you did not get the position and wealth by walking God's way, then the only thing you will have is heartache and sorrow. **Matthew 6:33** is still in the Bible, and God still commands us to seek Him before we seek anything. If we must choose between going to church or working a job, we ought to go to church. If we must choose between a high paying job and the will of God then we should choose the will of God over the high paying job. I fear that in our society today we have lost this truth that God's way always comes before position or wealth. Now if in walking God's way, position and wealth come, there is nothing wrong with this, but if we seek position and wealth by forsaking God's way then it matters not what position we obtain or how much wealth we get, it is wrong.

2. He did not let his physical weaknesses stop him in life.

In **Exodus 4:10-11**, we read **"And Moses said unto the LORD, O my Lord, I am not eloquent, neither heretofore, nor since thou hast spoken unto thy servant: but I am slow of speech, and of a slow tongue. And the LORD said unto him, Who hath made man's mouth? or who maketh the dumb, or deaf, or the seeing, or the blind? have not I the LORD?"** We learn that one of the physical weaknesses of Moses was that he did not talk clearly; he had a problem with stuttering. You can see in this verse that at first he did not think that God could use him with this weakness, and yet later on, we see that after he got it settled in his mind that God could still use him, he went forward. Moses did not let his speech impediment stop him from being used of God.

We must realize that with any of the weaknesses that we have, God made us the way we are and because He made us that way, He can use us in that condition. We should never question whether God can use us in the condition we are in, but we should instead trust an all-knowing God who knows what is best and can use us the way He made us. If God can use a donkey to preach a sermon to a backslidden preacher

9

by the name of Balaam, then certainly God can use us even with the weaknesses and frailties that we may have. Never let your physical weaknesses be the excuse that keeps you from serving God.

3. He kept a good relationship with his family.

Exodus 4:18, "And Moses went and returned to Jethro his father in law, and said unto him, Let me go, I pray thee, and return unto my brethren which are in Egypt, and see whether they be yet alive. And Jethro said to Moses, Go in peace."

Throughout the life of Moses we see that he kept a good relationship with his father-in-law. You will even find later on in the book of Exodus that it was Jethro, his father-in-law, who had come for a visit, and while visiting, he saw the pressure that Moses was under and he advised Moses to delegate some of his duties to other men so that he would not wear himself out. Moses and his father-in-law were on good terms with each other. Aaron was his brother and assistant in the ministry, and we even see later on that Miriam, his sister, was also involved and had a decent relationship with Moses.

How important it is in the Christian life that we keep good relationships with our family. We ought to constantly work on having a good relationship with our parents and with our siblings. We should never go through life being at odds with our family. We only have one family and we ought to do our best to get along with them. God says in **Proverbs 17:17, "A friend loveth at all times, and a brother is born for adversity."** There is going to come a time in your life that you are going to need your family and you had better be careful not to burn so many bridges with your family that one day you will be all alone because you have never done anything to keep a good relationship with them. What a shame that children cannot get along with their parents! One day you will wish you had a good relationship and unless you start working on it now, you will regret it later on in life.

Not only should you try to have a good relationship with your immediate family, but you should also do everything in your power to have a good relationship with your in-laws. I know there are plenty of good jokes out there about mothers-in-law, but honestly, God has given me the best in-laws in the world. I believe we ought to work hard at keeping a good relationship with our in-laws.

4. He understood that compromise never gives what it promises.

In **Exodus 10:24-29**, we see one of the four compromises that Pharaoh had offered to Moses in letting them go to serve God. Yet in each of these compromises that were offered, Moses knew that if he would give in one time, he would lose the battle. He understood that compromise never gives you what it promises, so the best thing to do is never compromise.

Likewise the same is true for every Christian. We need to realize that compromising God's commands should never be an option. You see, once Satan gets us to move one time then he knows that he can get us to move a second time. If we never give in the first time then we never have to worry about giving in the second time. We should never compromise for the sake of getting along with people or for the sake of having a bigger church, for we may compromise what we believe in and eventually, we will become something different from what we are right now. Compromising changes us from what we are right now to something that we have always been against in the past. So when the Devil comes to offer us a compromise we should, like Moses, be determined to do only what God has commanded us to do. We should claim the song, "I shall not be, I shall not be moved" and make this song the foundation upon which we deal with Satan.

5. He was not easily discouraged.

In **Exodus 32:11-14**, the children of Israel had just committed the great sin of setting up the golden calf and now God tells Moses to step away from the people so that He can destroy them and then make of him a great nation. Moses intercedes to God for the people and asks God not to destroy them for His name's sake. Moses told God that if He was to destroy them then all the heathen nations would think that God did not have enough power to bring them through the wilderness and that His name would be scoffed at among the heathen. God listened to Moses and did not destroy Israel as he had planned. Over and over Moses had to face these times that could have easily discouraged him, but instead, Moses came out on top of the circumstances of life and would not let these circumstances discourage him. This is most likely one of the reasons why he was a great leader.

Great leaders cannot be easily discouraged. If you are going to be a great leader then you cannot let things and circumstances get you down. If you are going to be the leader of the home, men, then you cannot be easily discouraged and lead the home in the right direction. Your home will not follow you if you let everything get you down. Likewise, ladies, if you are going to be the leader who your children need you to be then you cannot let the circumstances of life get you discouraged. Yes, we all must face adverse circumstances, but great leaders are not easily discouraged. Leaders must show restraint in times of hardship and not let the problems of life get them down.

6. He had an intimate relationship with God.

Notice in **Exodus 33:11** where it says, **"And the LORD spake unto Moses face to face, as a man speaketh unto his friend."** Again in **Exodus 34:29**, the Bible says, **"And it came to pass, when Moses came down from mount Sinai with the two tables of testimony in Moses' hand, when he came down from the mount, that Moses wist not that the**

skin of his face shone while he talked with him." Moses as a Christian and as a leader knew the importance of having an intimate relationship with God. He walked so close to God that God felt comfortable talking to him face to face. Moses spent so much time with God that it says that the skin of Moses' face shined with the glory of God. You see, Moses walked so much with God that he began to have the shine of God upon his countenance.

An intimate relationship with God will produce a change in your countenance. You will not have to tell people how much you walk with God for your countenance will reveal your walk with God. It says in **Exodus 34:35** that Moses' face shined so much with God's glory that he had to cover his face when he talked to the people. If you are having a problem with how people perceive you then I would advise that you start walking with God. This will most certainly change the way people perceive you. I mean, when is the last time someone has come to you and knew you were a Christian without you telling them? If you spend much time with God, most certainly your countenance will portray the countenance of God so that people will be able to look at you and see that you have been with God.

7. He realized that obstacles were only opportunities to show God's power.

Look at Moses in **Exodus 14:13**, where he stands at the Red Sea as the armies of Pharaoh are coming after him. The children of Israel were scared and afraid and all they could see was a body of water in front of them. However, Moses saw the obstacle of the Red Sea as an opportunity for God to show His power. Moses said in this verse, **"...Fear ye not, stand still, and see the salvation of the LORD, which he will shew to you to day: for the Egyptians whom ye have seen to day, ye shall see them again no more for ever."** Moses did not fret over the opportunity, but instead, he realized that he was about to see God's hand work in a miraculous way. And did he ever see God's hand work!

13

Again they were in the wilderness without water with only a bunch of rocks around them and the people began to murmur about not having any water. Did Moses get worried over this? No! He went to God realizing this obstacle of no water in sight was an opportunity for God to show His mighty power again, and God gave water from the rock.

We must realize that obstacles are opportunities turned inside out. We must not fret and worry about the obstacles of life, but we must realize that God placed those obstacles there so that we could see His power in our life. We must run to God as Moses did and let God show us His power. An obstacle can only stop us if all we do is murmur as the people did. We must be a people who look at obstacles as opportunities for God to work through us. Obstacles should excite us instead of depressing us, for these obstacles are divinely placed by God in our paths for us to see and be reminded of His mighty power.

8. When others were negative, he found a way to be positive.

In **Numbers 14:5-10**, the twelve spies had come back from spying out the land of Canaan and ten of those spies came back with a negative report. Yet in this passage of Scripture, Moses, Aaron, Joshua and Caleb all found a way to be positive though everyone around them was being negative. Instead of them looking at the iron chariots, the walled cities and the giants of the land, they looked at the grapes of Eschol and the prosperity that the land had, and most importantly, the God who promised that land to them.

You will never rise to the top by being negative. You check out the great leaders of life and see how many of them were negative. You won't find great leaders being negative, for people don't want to follow negative people. Society is negative enough without our leaders being negative. If your home is going to rise to the top, you must find a way to be positive when others are negative. If your church is going to rise to the top, you must find a way to be positive when others are negative. If your business is going to rise to the top, you must find a way to be positive when others are negative. If you as an individual are going to rise to the top in society, you must be positive in life and avoid the negatives. Anybody can be negative, but only great leaders and great people can find the positive in a negative situation.

9. He never abused his power.

Oh, the importance that we learn this from Moses. When Aaron and Miriam attacked him about the woman who he married, he did not use his position to get back at them. On the other hand, the Bible says that he was a very meek man. Meekness is simply power under control. He never abused his powers of being a leader and this is why God defended him.

Great leaders never use position for their gain, but they use their position to help their followers grow and profit. Your purpose of having position is not to see what you can get because of that position; your purpose of having position is to help those whom you lead. If you seek position so that you can gain from those whom you lead, you are seeking position for the wrong reason. Moses knew the importance of not abusing his position, and we also would be wise in learning this same characteristic.

10. He did not let his shortcomings stop him.

In **Numbers 20:12-14**, Moses made that great mistake in his life by smiting the rock instead of speaking to the rock like God had told him. Because of his disobedience to God, he would now not be able to enter into the Promised Land. Yet in verse 14, I love what it says, after he had just been chastened by God and told that he would not enter into the Promised Land, this verse says, **"And Moses sent..."** Moses did not let a mistake in his life stop him from serving God or going forward in life.

Let's just be honest with each other. None of us is perfect in life and all of us will make mistakes in life, but we cannot let the mistakes that we make in life stop us from serving God. There is still life to live and we must not think that God cannot still use us. So, you have made a mistake or even messed your life up in sin; don't let your shortcoming stop you in life from serving God. Don't add to your sin by quitting on God but go forward and realize that God can still use you, but you must get up and keep going as Moses did.

11. He was a soul winner.

Numbers 21:9 is the story of Moses lifting up the brazen serpent in the wilderness. Everyone who looked to this brazen serpent when they were bitten by the snakes would be healed. Moses knew that he must lift that brazen serpent so that others could be saved from the bite of sin.

Likewise, we must be like Moses and lift up Christ to a dying world. We must go out to a lost and dying world and show them that the only hope of them making it through the bite of sin is to look to Christ. Every Christian should be a soul winner! We must live our lives pointing people to Christ, realizing there are millions of people who are dying in sin and someone like Moses must lift up Christ so that the world can see Him and live.

12. He did not let old age stop him or slow him down.

I like what **Deuteronomy 34:7** says, **"And Moses was an hundred and twenty years old when he died: his eye was not dim, nor his natural force abated."** Even when Moses was old, he still served God. It says in this verse that he was 120 years old and still going strong for God. He never let his age slow him down or stop him from serving God. He died as an old man still serving God like when he was a young man.

16

Never let your age be an excuse for not doing something for God, whether young or old. Far too many times in this world we have people using their age to say that they are too old to do anything for God. What a shame that we would use our age as an excuse to be lazy on God! I understand you may not have the strength and energy like you used to have, but this is not an excuse for you to do nothing for God. If you are still alive and breathing air on this planet then God expects you to serve Him. God's plan for your life is not done until He decides to take you home to Heaven. Never use your age as an excuse but instead ask God to give you the strength to continue to serve Him. It should be said about all of us when we die that our "natural force" was not abated when it came to serving God. Keep your zeal for serving God and serve Him with the strength that you do have.

13. He prepared for the next generation.

In **Numbers 27:22-23**, God tells Moses to prepare Joshua to take over for him after he is gone on to Heaven. God was teaching through the life of Moses the importance of training people for the next generation. Moses spent the remainder of his life training Joshua to carry on what he had done for many years.

All Christians should be like Moses and live their lives preparing for the next generation. We should never come to the end of our life and not have left something for the next generation. The next generation should have been trained so well by us that they have something to pass on to the next generation. As I write this chapter I am sitting on the airplane flying to my mother's funeral. I can honestly say that she prepared for the next generation by instilling in me the principles from the Bible that I am now trying to pass on to the next generation. She spent her life passing on to me and many others what was given to her by previous generations. She prepared us and taught us so that when she was gone, we could carry on and continue to give to future generations what was given to her. We all should prepare the generation

17

that follows us to carry on to the next generation that follows them the fundamentals of the faith and the methods of the faith that were given to us.

This man Moses was more than just a great leader and probably the greatest human leader of all time; he was a great Christian! Every one of us would be wise to look at the attributes of the life of Moses and emulate these attributes in our life.

2

Good Success

Joshua 1:8, "This book of the law shall not depart out of thy mouth; but thou shalt meditate therein day and night, that thou mayest observe to do according to all that is written therein: for then thou shalt make thy way prosperous, and then thou shalt have good success."

One of the favorite stories of children in the Bible is the story of Joshua leading the children of Israel around the walls of Jericho until they crumbled, and he and the people went in and conquered the strongest city in Canaan at that time. What a great story to read about! For six days, they walked around the city of Jericho and said nothing; on the seventh day they walked around the city seven times, blew their trumpets and shouted, and those huge walls came crumbling down. What a site that must have been! What an experience these people were part of! Yet, the truth is, this would have never happened had Joshua not followed several key principles to make him into the man and leader that he became. Let me explain.

Joshua was born in the land of Egypt during the time that the children of Israel were in bondage to the Egyptians. He saw how Pharaoh treated the people and he saw the wickedness of this Pharaoh who tried to have the men children killed. But he also saw how a man by the name of Moses rose to prominence among the children of Israel and became their leader. He watched Moses with God's hand upon him approach Pharaoh without fear and demand to let the people go so that they may serve God. He saw Pharaoh refuse to let the people go and then he saw how God sent the plagues upon the Egyptians and not upon the children of Israel. Joshua had seen all of this! Then, he was part of the great plague that the Bible calls the Passover. For this plague, God commanded Moses and Israel to kill the firstborn lamb, take that lamb's blood, and apply it upon the doorposts of their houses. That night, a death angel was to pass over Egypt and whoever did not have the blood applied would have the firstborn male in their homes killed. Joshua was there when this great plague happened and he heard the wails of parents and children as they saw the firstborn males in their families die. He was also part of fleeing Egypt, seeing God part that great Red Sea and destroying the whole Egyptian army. Joshua was one of the twelve spies who went into Canaan land to search it out and bring a report back to Moses about what he saw. Yet, he was only one of two men who brought back a good report and not an evil one. Joshua, for forty years, followed at the footsteps of Moses, was his minister and was part of all the great miracles in the wilderness.

Now, Moses has died and Joshua became the leader of Israel. How intimidating this must have been to have to follow such a great man of God like Moses. Now it was his time to take the leadership role and to take the children of Israel into the Promised Land in order to receive the inheritance that God had promised to his people several hundred years prior. Joshua accomplished what God had set him up to do. At the end of his life, you see that most of the land of Canaan had been conquered and the children of Israel had complete control of all their enemies.

As we study the life of Joshua, we can see that there are several keys to the success of Joshua. These keys helped him to become the man and leader that he was. I believe these same keys will help us to be victorious and successful in our life as we serve God and do His will. Let me give you the keys that helped Joshua become not just a success, but as **Joshua 1:8** says, a **"good success."**

1. He got God on his side.

Look at **Joshua 1:5, "There shall not any man be able to stand before thee all the days of thy life: as I was with Moses, so I will be with thee: I will not fail thee, nor forsake thee."** Notice that it says that as God was with Moses, He would also be with Joshua. How important it was to get God on his side! I don't believe that God just all of a sudden decided to put the blessing of His presence upon the life of Joshua. I believe that God watched Joshua as a young man. He followed the footsteps of his leader Moses, and when his friends were out playing, he was by the man of God learning from him. God saw this and God decided that there was no better man to take over after Moses than this man Joshua, who had walked with Moses and no doubt had walked with God as he learned from Moses. God was simply telling Joshua in this verse that just because Moses had passed away and was now in Heaven that did not mean God was also gone. Though the great man of God, Moses, was gone, his God was still there. Joshua did not have to fear that God had left him. Joshua got God on his side several years before Moses died, and God was assuring him that He would still be with him as He was with Moses.

If we are ever going to be successful in doing God's will for our life then we also must realize that we need to get God on our side. You see, when God is on your side then it matters not who is against you, for victory is yours. In **Romans 8:31** it says, **"...If God be for us, who can be against us?"** It does not matter how big the opponent is; when God is on your side, you are guaranteed a victory, for who can stand against God? Again in **Romans 8:37** the Bible says, **"Nay, in all these things we are more than conquerors through him that loved us."** When God is on your side, you will be a conqueror. **1 John 4:4** says, **"...greater is he that is in you, than he that is in the world."** Getting God on your side is the most important thing a Christian can ever do; for if He is not for you then that would mean He is against you and no one can win when God is against him. As Joshua got God on his side by doing right and following the man of God, we also will get God on our side and get God to fight for us by doing right, living right and following the man of God.

2. He did not listen to his fears.

As I have said previously in this chapter, how intimidating this must have been for Joshua to take the role of leadership and follow such a great man like Moses. I can only imagine how he felt inside as he wondered how he would ever get the people to follow him. Just think of this, Moses was a great man and Joshua had pretty much grown up with all the people whom he is to now lead. I am sure he thought to himself that he could never be Moses. This thought would have been true, if he thought this, because there was and will only be one Moses. However, God made him whom he was and made him for this time in order to lead the children of Israel into the Promised Land. If he was going to be successful in doing God's will for his life, then he had to ignore his fears and realize that God is the One Who made him to do this job. This is why God said in **Joshua 1:6, "Be strong and of a good courage..."** Again in **Joshua 1:7,** God said to Joshua, **"Only be thou strong and very courageous..."** God knew that if Joshua was going to be successful then he must not listen to his fear. He must be strong and courageous and do what God had called him to do in spite of his fears.

However, in any endeavor in life there is the possibility of failure. If you are going to be a success, you cannot cower because of the fear of failure. You must be strong, courageous and go after what God has called you to do. You cannot let the fear of failure stop you! The only difference between the successful person and the mediocre person is their response to fear. The successful person has fears just like the mediocre person has fears, but the successful person will not listen to their fears. The mediocre person has fears, and they listen to their fears; they end up not doing anything because of their fear of failure. Christian, you are going to fail in life if you endeavor to do anything, but you cannot let your fear of failure stop you from pursuing what God has called you to do. Eighteen years ago I stepped out into full-time evangelism. Truthfully, I was afraid, but I would not listen to these fears. Now, eighteen years later, I am still preaching the Gospel of Christ all over this country and even to parts of the world. If I would have listened to my fears, I think I would still be working a full-time job and would have never been satisfied in life. Successful people cannot listen to their fears. Whatever your fear is, that is natural, but you must plug your ears to your fears, step out and do what God has called and made you to do.

3. He spent time with God.

Notice in **Joshua 1:8** it says, **"This book of the law shall not depart out of thy mouth; but thou shalt meditate therein day and night..."** Joshua knew the importance of spending time with God. He knew that if he was to become successful and stay successful then he would have to spend time with his God. Every great man in the Bible whom God used was used mainly because he spent time with God everyday.

That is what this verse is teaching when it says that we are to meditate on the Bible day and night. In order to meditate on something, you have to spend time reading about it. That means there was a specific time for them to read and then again a specific time to meditate or think about the Bible. God told Joshua that he was to meditate or think about the Bible every day and night. This most certainly would be one of the most important keys to Joshua staying successful. He had seen how Moses had spent time with God daily and if he was going to keep God on his side, then he also must spend time with God daily.

Never has a person been successful in the will of God without spending time with God. As I have studied great men of the Bible and great men of God from the past, every one of them had a personal time with God; everyday they read His Word and talked to Him in prayer. One of the greatest failures of

23

Christians today is that we just don't spend time with God. We wonder why we live in a powerless generation with nothing happening in our churches or even in our lives, and the truth is that we just don't spend time with God as we should. Great Christians spend a great amount of time with God. Backslidden, cold, and defeated Christians spend little or no time with God. Whenever I counsel someone who is struggling with the will of God for their life, I always ask them how much time they are spending with God. Without spending time with God, you are sure to fail. You will never know how to do God's will properly without spending time with God, for God will tell you how to do His will.

4. He set goals.

In **Joshua 1:11** it says, **"...Prepare you victuals: for within three days ye shall pass over this Jordan..."** Joshua was a man who believed in setting goals. It says in **"three days ye shall pass over."** What was this? This was a goal! They had a goal that in three days they were going over Jordan. Joshua set many goals in his life. He had a goal to make it through the wilderness, and he did. He had a goal to get over the Jordan River, and he did. He had a goal to get into the Promised Land, and he did. He set goals to conquer the cities of Canaan for God's sake. He conquered most of these cities. There were only a few left that he had not conquered by the time of his death. Yes, he did not accomplish all of his goals, but he would have never accomplished any of his goals if he had not set some goals to pursue.

If you are going to be successful in the Christian life or even life in general, then you must set goals. Goals give you directions of where to go, and without any goals in life, you will go nowhere. You are sure to hit your target if you have no goals for there is nothing at which to aim. Oh, you may fail in hitting your target if you set goals, but you will have progressed much farther in life with goals than without goals. You see, I would rather aim high and miss it than to aim at nothing and hit it. If my goals are high and I miss those goals

24

then I am higher than I was without any goals. But if I have no goals and aim at nothing then I am sure to hit my target: nothing. Without goals, you really become a nothing in life because you are shooting at nothing.

Goals are the end zone of life, and they let you know whether you have scored or not. Without goals, you are sure to lose in the game of life. Could you imagine a football game without an end zone? Whether you make it into the end zone or not, at least you know how much farther you have to go. Likewise, life needs goals to let us know how we are progressing. If you are going to be successful in doing what God's will is for your life then you must be someone who sets goals and then pursues those goals. Every husband should have goals for his marriage! Every parent should have goals for their children! Every Christian should have goals for their Christian life! Every pastor should have goals for his church! Every ministry worker should have goals for their ministry! Every business person should have goals for their business! Every person in general should set goals, for goals will help you to go forward. They are what motivate us to accomplish things in life for God. Without goals you will be in ten years exactly where you are right now.

5. He was a producer.

Notice in **Joshua 1:8** it says, "**...then thou shalt make thy ways prosperous, and then thou shalt have good success.**" Joshua knew the importance of being a producer in life and not just a maintainer. He knew that producing meant that he accomplished something, and that is truly important if we are going to be successful.

Successful people are people who produce and accomplish things in life. There are thousands of people who are busy in life, but there are few people who produce in life. Now, let me just be honest with you; God created us and made us to produce! All through the Bible you see God's commands are for us to go forward and to reproduce after ourselves. God

25

never intended for anybody to be a free loader in life. God intended for everyone to pay their own way through life.

In your church, are you the one who is producing people down the aisle or are you the one who only fills a spot during the service times? Christians are to be producers! Oh, you may be very busy doing things in the church, but the ultimate goal of every Christian should be to be a producer by going out and seeing people saved and bringing them to church to get baptized. If you are on staff for someone, you are on that staff to produce and not to maintain. If all you do is maintain and not produce then you are a failure! You were not hired just to maintain a position. Anybody can do this. You were hired to produce and make your hiring worthwhile. Those who move up in life, whether in the Christian life or even in the business world, are people who are producers. Producers will always move to the top because their works alone push them higher, and eventually, they will become the leaders of that in which they are involved.

6. He prepared ahead of time.

In **Joshua 1:11** we see the phrase, **"...prepare you victuals..."** Joshua was a man who prepared ahead of time. In order to go through the Jordan River, he had to prepare to go through that river. In order to conquer Jericho and Canaan Land, he had to be a man who prepared. He would have never made it if he was not a man who prepared ahead of time. Joshua knew the importance of preparation because preparation is what allowed him to be able to handle each battle that came his way and handle the problems of that battle. Without preparation, Joshua would have never made it into the Promised Land.

We must realize that great leaders learn to prepare ahead of time. God teaches us all through the Bible of the importance of preparing ahead of time. He tells us in **Proverbs 6:6-8, "Go to the ant, thou sluggard; consider her ways, and be wise: Which having no guide, overseer, or ruler,**

Provideth her meat in the summer, and gathereth her food in the harvest." God shows us through the example of the ant about the importance of preparing or planning ahead of time. Preparation keeps the crisis moments at a minimum. If you are a person who never plans ahead then I would imagine that you are a person who lives quite often in a crisis. Joshua knew how important it was to prepare ahead of time. We also should realize that our success in life leans quite heavily on how much we prepare ahead of time.

7. He did not try to be smarter than history.

In **Joshua 1:13** the Bible says that Joshua was to **"Remember the word which Moses…commanded you…"** Joshua certainly did this! He never thought that he knew more than Moses did; instead, all he did was copy what Moses did. It made Moses successful, and he knew it was sure to make him successful.

History can be the greatest teacher in life. You see, history has no axes to grind other than to tell you what has worked and what has not worked. We would be wise in our lives to not think that we can outsmart history and get by with something that others could not. We would be wise to simply copy what has made others successful instead of changing the methods that were given to us from the past only for the sake of creating our own niche to impress people.

One of the biggest culprits of compromise is when an individual is so consumed with "being their own man" that they forsake the methods of great men of the past and try to carve a new path to walk. This is one of the biggest reasons America is in the shape that she is in today. We have forsaken what has made America great for the sake of political correctness and for the sake of not offending people, and in so doing, we are destroying our nation. I see churches in our generation doing this same thing. We have changed the methods of great men of the past to copy the "new" ways because we live in a different age. Ladies and gentlemen, let

27

me emphatically say it matters not in what century we live; the methods and procedures of those from the past still work today. We don't need to look for new methods or new ways to do things. We just need to copy what those from the past did who were successful, and we should do the same. Joshua certainly knew that he was not smarter than history, and neither are we!

8. He followed the proper roles of authority.

Joshua was a man who knew what the proper roles of authority were, and he followed them. When he was the servant of Moses, we never see him going around Moses or questioning Moses. No, he followed the proper role of authority. When he became the leader of the children of Israel, he followed the proper roles of authority, as we see in **Joshua 1:17**. He knew what his position was and he knew that he was under God; therefore he followed that role of authority.

Following authority does not make you a weak person, but instead, it makes you a stronger person. If you don't learn to follow authority when you are a follower then you will be a poor leader if you ever get the opportunity to lead. Great leaders and successful leaders learn the importance of following authority. We must not fall to Satan's tactics of questioning authority, but we must follow God's methods of submitting to authority. If you ever rise to a high position in life, your potential in that position will only rise to the height that you learned to follow authority when you were a follower.

9. He did not spend time with rebels.

As we follow the life of Joshua, we see that he never sided with the rebels but always sided with those who were following God and the man of God.

The quickest way to destroy everything that you have built in your life is to associate yourself with rebels. Rebels will

28

destroy you and bring you down. By nature, a rebel is a destroyer. You may succeed in life, but the length of your success will be determined by how much you choose to associate with rebels.

Joshua was most certainly successful in life. In fact, the word success only occurs one time in the Bible and that is in the book of Joshua. If we are going to be successful in life then we are going to be successful on purpose. Most of our success is determined by what we do before we reach the position that we will fill for the rest of our life. Every Christian should look at the life of Joshua and copy the keys that led him to success. These keys will work for us just like they did for Joshua. Don't be guilty of looking at this great life and then let the life that he lived be only a story to you. Instead make it a blueprint to follow this man who, from his youth to his death, served God and never waivered in doing the will of God for his life.

3

The Friend of God

Isaiah 41:8, "But thou, Israel, art my servant, Jacob whom I have chosen, the seed of Abraham my friend."

When God described to us whom Abraham was, He said that Abraham was the friend of God. What a special relationship these two must have had for God to call Abraham His friend. Nowhere in the entire Bible will you find God calling anyone else His friend: only Abraham.

When Abraham was born, he was given the name Abram which means "high father." Abraham was to be the father of Israel. The main emphasis on the life of Abraham was that he had no children and yet he trusted and believed that God was going to make him the father of many nations. He was considered a great man of faith because he left his homeland at the command of God, without any children, to go to a land that he had never seen, to be the father of many nations as God promised him he would become. This took faith, for he left a place where he was highly successful in the eyes of man. He left everything to become the father of many nations, yet he had no sign that he was going to be that father other than God's promise to him. Even when God changed his name from Abram to Abraham, which means "father of many nations," he never lost sight and hope of the promise of God to him. It was not until he was one hundred years old that he had Isaac who was to be the son that would carry on the promise from God. Imagine all of those years, he believed in the promise even when it seemed physically impossible for him to have any children. Yet, though all of those years passed by, he never gave up on God. Maybe it was because of his undying faith that God called him His friend. Whatever the reason, we can learn several lessons from the life of Abraham.

1. God cannot use you until you burn your bridges to the past.

God told Abraham in **Genesis 12:1-2** that he was to leave his country, his kindred, his father's house and homeland to go to a land where God would make of him a great nation. Notice he was to leave everything before God would bless him and start using him. The reason for this is that God wanted to see if Abraham had enough faith in Him to burn his bridges to everything that he knew in order for God to use him. This burning of bridges to the past, for Abraham, was the beginning of a life of faith in God. It was this burning of bridges that proved to God that Abraham did have faith that God could do something through him. The blessing of God on Abraham's life would never have happened if he would not have stepped out by faith and left everything for God's sake. It was this act of faith that put God's blessings upon his life.

We need to realize that God cannot use us until we burn our bridges to the past. Far too many times we try to hang onto something just in case serving God does not work out. This is not faith. When you burn your bridges and leave no way to go back to the past you are saying, sink or swim, it is now God and me on this journey. This certainly takes faith.

I recall when I stepped out into full-time evangelism; I had a total of four meetings on my schedule. I quit my job and went full-time into evangelism trusting that God would take care of me, and for these eighteen years He has done just that. Why? Because God honors those who step out by faith and burn their bridges to the past and say, "I am going one direction and that is forward." You see, the reason God blesses this is because this is faith. God says in **Hebrews 11:6, "But without faith it is impossible to please him: for he that cometh to God must believe that he is, and that he is a rewarder of them that diligently seek him."** The only

31

way that anyone can please God is through faith, and it takes a lot of faith in God to burn your bridges to the past! You see, when you burn bridges to the past you are proving to God that you believe Him and that you are going to trust Him over any possession or link to the past. Without this type of faith, the type of faith that causes you to burn bridges to the past, God cannot and will not use you to your fullest potential. It is only when we put our whole trust in God that He will then decide to use us. The one way we can prove that we have put our whole trust in God is to burn our bridges to the past.

No man of God will be used in a great way until he burns his bridges to the past and decides to make it work where God has called him. No college student will be used of God in Bible College until they burn their bridges to home and say, "I am going to stick it out and make it. Running home is not the answer. God is the answer." Any person who ever has a desire to be used by God in a great way must burn those bridges to the past, cut the apron strings to mama and decide to do what God has told them to do instead of what daddy or mama has told them to do. Your first requirement to be used by God is to burn your bridges!

2. You will always pick up baggage when traveling in the world.

Notice in **Genesis 12:10** that during a time of famine the Bible says that Abraham **"…went down into Egypt to sojourn there…"** He went there just because there was a famine in the land. Now it is interesting that Abraham had enough faith to give up everything to go to this land that God had promised to him and yet did not have enough faith that God would take care of him in a time of famine. Because of his lack of faith in God during this time, he decided to go and sojourn in the land of Egypt. The word "sojourn" in this verse means "to pass through." All Abraham said that he was going to do was pass through the land of Egypt and then come back to where God wanted him to be. Egypt, as many of us know, is a type of the world. Abraham planned to only pass through the world, but notice, while passing through he stayed for awhile and ended up hiring a little maid whose name was Hagar. This little journey that he took caused him to pick up a piece of baggage from Egypt that has truthfully caused much turmoil to Abraham and to the people of Israel to this day.

You must learn that you will never just pass through the world without staying in the world for awhile. Many a person has just wanted to pass through the world and see what the world was like, but I have news for you, anytime you go window shopping in the world you will end up buying something from the world. Whatever you pick up from the world, you will find that it will never satisfy you as much as you thought that it would.

As you may know, I travel somewhere just about every week of my life to go and preach in revival meetings or conferences. In these eighteen years of traveling, I have yet to go to a place without having to buy something from that place. The majority of these times I am simply passing through these places for a few days, yet every time I end up getting something from that place. Likewise, the same is true with the world! As much as you try to just pass through the world, you will always pick up something that you had not planned on picking up. That something becomes a piece of undesirable luggage that you have to haul around in life, all because you were just going to pass through the world. Christian, why not learn from the life of Abraham and realize that you will never just pass through the world without staying for a while, and while passing through the world you will always pick up baggage while in the world? Our best bet is to simply not pass through the world if we don't want any luggage from the world.

3. You will never get right with God without an altar.

Abraham now figured out that the world, Egypt, never gave him what he thought that it would, and now Abraham wanted to come back to God. He knew that if he was going to come back to God, and get right with God, then he must go back to the place where he had been at the beginning which was Bethel, the house of God, and get right with God at the altar in Bethel. It says in **Genesis 13:3-4, "And he went on his journeys from the south even to Bethel, unto the place where his tent had been at the beginning, between Bethel and Hai; Unto the place of the altar, which he had made there at the first: and there Abram called on the name of the LORD."** It was at the altar where Abraham got right with God, and it was the altar at the house of God.

The same is true for you and me. If we are going to get right with God, we first of all must come up out of the world and then get back to the altar. It is at the altar where God expects for us to get things right with Him. We will never get right with God without an altar. This is certainly one of the biggest problems we see in Christianity today. Christianity has lost the importance of using the altar at the church. You go to the average church and look at the altar during the invitation, that is, if they have one, and see how full these altars are. How sad it is to see altars empty in our churches today. We wonder why churches are dead. It is because we have far too many worldly Christians who never use an altar and never get right with God. No wonder we see sin destroying lives. No wonder we see churches dying. Why? Because the altars have been forsaken! Until we get back to using the altars in our churches we cannot expect to have a good relationship with God. I care not how good you think you are, everyone should use the altar! The truth is, the closer you get to God the more you will use the altar. As you get closer to God, His righteousness will shine a light on your unrighteousness and this will cause you to use the altar if you want to be right with God.

People say quite often, "Well, why should I use the altar if God has not touched my heart?" The only thing they are doing is revealing how far they are from God! The closer to God they are the more they will see their need for the altar. You will notice in this instance in Abraham's life that God did not speak to Abraham's heart. No, it was God's righteousness that had revealed to Abraham his need to go back to the altar. God's righteousness had revealed to Abraham his unrighteousness. Many times we are waiting for God to speak to us when in all reality God does not have to speak to us all the time for us to go to an altar. Many times if we will just get close enough to God to let His righteousness shine a light on our heart, His righteousness will reveal to us our unrighteousness, and this is why we must use the altar. Again I say, without an altar you will never get right with God.

4. Sin always causes strife.

Now Abraham had just gotten right with God and you would think that everything would be fine, but we see the opposite is true. In **Genesis 13:7** the Bible says, **"And there was a strife between the herdmen of Abram's cattle and the herdmen of Lot's cattle…"** What was the strife between these two families and their herdsman? It was a result of the sin that Abraham had committed by going down to Egypt. It was his journey down to Egypt that exposed Lot to the world, and now, though Abraham had returned to God, Lot was still in his backslidden state. This strife was the direct result of sin.

Sin will always cause strife in our lives. It will cause strife with us as a person. It will cause strife with our family members whom we live with. It will also cause strife with others with whom we associate. Sin never brings peace. Sin always causes strife. Sin never leads to a peaceful life. It only leads to a life of turmoil and strife that will most certainly follow us until we get right, and many times, for years after we get right. Not only does sin cause strife to us as an individual, but it will also cause strife to those whom we love. Our sin makes our loved ones pay for what we have done. Trust me when I say this, sin has long fingers and those fingers reach farther than you could ever imagine. Wherever the fingers of sin reach, you can count on it that it will cause strife in the life of the one it reaches.

Christian, why do you think that your sin will not hurt you or others around you? Sin has always and will always affect us. We are never above the price of sin and sin will always cause strife in our lives. This is why we must not partake of the sin that our flesh wants us to partake, for it will bring strife to our life. Just look at history and look at those who promote sin and tell me it won't cause any strife. It most certainly will, and it most certainly does. Sin is never peaceful; sin is always filled with strife.

5. Always do right no matter how others have treated you.

Abraham, in **Genesis 14:14**, heard that Lot his nephew had been taken captive. Abraham took his servants to rescue Lot from the hands of his captors. You have to understand, Lot had treated Abraham very wrongly and yet Abraham was still treating Lot in a right way and a Christian way. Why? Because Abraham knew that you always do right no matter what others have done to you.

Just because someone else has done you wrong, it does not give you a license to do wrong back to them. No, the Christian thing to do is found in **Matthew 5:44** where it says to, **"Love your enemies, bless them that curse you, do good to them that hate you, and pray for them which despitefully use you, and persecute you;"** I am to always do right no matter how others have treated me. My treatment of others is not to be dependent upon what they have done for me, but dependent upon what God has commanded us to do to others and that is to do good to them even when they have treated us wrong.

I realize that doing good to others may not seem natural and doing good to others may actually seem to be hard when we look at what they have done to us. But, I am more interested in God's blessings upon my life than them getting "what they deserve." Having the blessing of God on my life for doing right to others who have wronged me is more important to me than to get my revenge on that person or to rejoice when their day of trouble comes. I should realize that, like Abraham treated Lot right even when Lot had wronged him, I also should treat others right even when they have wronged me.

6. A lack of righteousness is the result of a lack of faith.

Notice in **Genesis 15:7** that it was Abraham's faith in God that was counted for righteousness. It was Abraham trusting God by faith that God was going to make his seed as the stars of the heaven which helped him to live a righteous life.

Any lack of faith in God in our lives can always be followed by a regression of righteous living. It is certainly worthy of noting that the more faith in God you have the more righteous you will live. Faith causes us to live righteously. If we have a lack of righteousness in our lives it is only because we have a lack of faith in our lives. It takes faith in God to live a righteous life, for living righteously is not easy, especially when we have not seen the fruit of our righteous living. It takes faith that God will reward us for living right. When your faith is weak in this area, then most likely your righteous living will also be weak.

7. Wrong leadership roles in the home will produce dysfunctional families.

Look at **Genesis 16:2** and you will see Sarah telling Abraham what he needs to do. This is contrary to the role of a wife in the home, according to the Bible. Sarah was trying to assume the wrong role of leadership in her home, and truthfully, Abraham allowed it to happen by listening to her. Oh, the heartache that was caused because of this wrong role of leadership in the home. This action caused a young child to be born whose name was Ishmael, and, oh, the heartache that this caused for this family. What it caused was a dysfunctional family for Ishmael. Now his father was not the husband of his mother, and look at the chaos it caused in both of these homes. This is what wrong roles of leadership in the

37

home will produce. It will produce families that are dysfunctional.

We wonder why we have so many dysfunctional homes in our society today and the reason is because we have homes where the proper roles of leadership are not being followed. You have women who won't submit to the leadership of their husbands. You have men who won't lead in the home and force the wife to lead. Then even worse, you have parents who won't lead in the home so the children take control of the home and lead. All of this causes dysfunctional homes. God never intended for the woman or the child to lead in the home. He intended for the man to be the leader in the home, and yet we have listened to political correctness and have ruined the homes in our society. Never in the history of this world have we had so many dysfunctional homes, and it can all be traced back to one thing, wrong roles of leadership in the home. If we are going to have the right type of home, then we must follow the proper roles of leadership which God set up from the beginning. God leads the husband, who leads the wife and following behind the wife you have the children who are obeying a mom and dad. Without these roles of leadership in the home the home will be dysfunctional.

8. Righteous living gives insights to life.

In **Genesis 18:19** God is talking to Himself about destroying the cities of Sodom and Gomorrah. God, as He discusses this matter, decides to show Abraham what He was going to do because He knew that Abraham lived a right life. It was because of the righteous living of Abraham that God gave him a special insight into what He was going to do.

When we live a righteous life it is a whole lot easier to see life through the eyes of God. You see, righteous living illumines the pathway of life. We see everything more clearly. When living righteously, our righteous living will always shine a brighter light on which path to go in life. When living a right life, you can make better decisions because your decision maker is able to see more clearly. The righteousness of God shining through you will give insight on the matter. Far more decisions in life could be made easier to make if we would live more righteous lives. Righteous living gives us better understanding of God's Word, which always will shine a brighter light on which pathway we should go in life. You will always find that the wisest and best counselors in life are those who live righteous lives.

9. Intercessory prayer can change the mind of God.

Oh how I love this lesson from Abraham's life! In **Genesis 18:23-33** we have the story of Abraham interceding with God to save the cities of Sodom and Gomorrah. We see Abraham in these verses literally bargaining with God to save these cities. You see, he was actually changing the mind of God by interceding on behalf of others. Notice that this prayer would have no effect on him. He did not get anything out of this prayer; this prayer was completely about others. It was his intercessory prayer for others that changed the mind of God.

We should realize that prayer should never be just about us, but prayer should include interceding for the needs of others. The good news we learn from this story is that our prayer life can change the mind of God. But what is even more important is that our prayer life should be a prayer life that intercedes for the sake of others so that God will change His mind concerning their situation or matters. Every nation needs some Christian who will intercede for it in such a way that if God is going to destroy it, this Christian could pray with such intercessory prayers that they could change the mind of God concerning that nation. Every individual needs someone who can intercede for them to God for God to meet their needs. The greatest prayers you can ever pray are not about you or your needs. The greatest prayers you can pray are intercessory prayers to God for the needs of others. We must never give up hope in our prayer life no matter how bleak the situation may look, for an intercessory prayer could change the mind of God.

10. God blesses an undying faith that never stops believing in the impossible.

We come now to the part of Abraham's life where his faith is finally rewarded. God in **Genesis 21:1-2** blesses Abraham and Sarah for never giving up on Him.

God always blesses faith, especially a faith that never stops believing that God can still perform the impossible. It matters not how impossible your situation may seem, your undying faith in God that He will come through will be rewarded. We must realize that the greater the test that faith endures, the greater the blessing and reward that faith receives. You don't think that Abraham and Sarah were happy when Isaac was born! I have news for you, even as hard as it may have been to have a child at their age, this child was proof to them, and to everyone that said they were crazy, that their faith was right. People may think you are crazy for having faith in God for something that may seem impossible, but if you will not let your faith die and keep believing that God will come through, when God does come through, it will certainly be rewarding. God knows when to come through and you must simply trust God that He knows when the best time is to reward your faith in Him. Until then, don't let your faith die and don't give up on God! Just keep on going forward and trusting God that He will come through.

11. Friendship to God can only be proven through total sacrifice.

In **Genesis 22:1** God comes to Abraham to test him. God asks Abraham if he would be willing to give his only son as a sacrifice to Him. You will notice in this verse it says that, **"God did tempt Abraham."** This does not mean that God was tempting him with wrong, but it was saying that God was testing Abraham, for that is what the word "tempt" means. What God was testing was Abraham's friendship to God. God wanted to see if there was anything that Abraham would hold back from Him or if there was anything that he would allow to come between him and God. Not only did Abraham have to give up his son, but he also had to persuade his wife that this was the right thing. I am very sure that Sarah had something to say about all of this. Yet Abraham came through this test with flying colors proving to God that there was nothing he would hold back from Him, and there was nothing that he would let come between him and his friendship to God.

This most certainly is the greatest test of one's friendship with God. It is always easy to be God's friend when you don't have to give up anything, but when God asks you to give up everything you have that is the true test of your friendship to God. Your friendship to God is never true unless it is tested. When you never have to give anything up to be a friend, then there is no test, for anyone can do this. But when you have to give up your most treasured possession in life to prove your friendship, and you still choose to be a friend, then this is when you have proven your friendship to God. If you say to God that you will not let anything come between you and Him and then God decides to test that, and if you stand true to your word, then you have proven to God that you are His friend. What is it that if God asked you to give it to Him that you would say "no" to God? Whatever that is, then that is your degree of friendship to God. It is not until you are willing to give everything you have to God, even if it is your most prized treasure, that your friendship to God will be proven.

12. Faith is justified by its work.

Now I am not saying that works are a part of salvation. This is the farthest from the truth! But faith is justified by our works. Abraham proved his faith to God in **Genesis 22:12** by being willing to offer his son to God as a sacrifice. It was his physical works that proved to God that Abraham believed that God would make of him a great nation.

Our works are our only way to prove to God that our faith is real. Several times in the Bible Jesus said, **"...when He saw**

41

their faith…" What was this? This was their works proving to God that they believed He could perform what He said He could do. Likewise it is only through our works that we can prove to God that we have the faith in Him to do whatever He says He can do. Many people can say, "I believe God can do the impossible", but only those who step out on the impossible will see the impossible. When God comes through for them, it is because their works justified, or better yet, proved that their faith was real. Without works you will not see the miracles in life from God that you could, because works justify your faith.

13. Obedience always produces blessings.

Notice now in **Genesis 22:18** we see that because Abraham had obeyed God, He was blessing Abraham by honoring the promise that He made to him many years prior.

Likewise, our obedience to God will always be followed by the blessings of God. If you ever want God's blessings on you, then the way to get His blessing upon you is to obey Him. Obedience always brings blessings. If you will just obey what He tells you to do, then you will see the blessings that He promises because of your obedience.

14. When you stop dreaming you stop living.

Abraham is now old, Sarah has now died, and Isaac is now a full grown man. Yet Isaac has not found a wife, and Abraham in **Genesis 22:1-4** commands his servant to go and find a wife for Isaac. His command to his servant was to not bring a wife back of the Canaanites. This young lady was to be from his kindred, for Abraham knew that the lineage of Christ was to come through his seed. Abraham, even in his old age, never lost the dream of being the father of many nations.

No matter what your age is, the day you stop dreaming is the day you begin to die. Show me a person with dreams and I will show you a person who is living. If you want to stay young and live, then never stop dreaming. As long as you have dreams to go after then you have a purpose for living. The day you lose your dreams is the day you lose your purpose for living, and that is the day you die inside. Even a person who is young yet has no dreams, though they may live many years after, is truthfully dead on the inside. Dreams are what keep you alive, therefore never stop dreaming.

15. Leave a heritage for your children to carry on.

Finally let me say, in **Genesis 25:5**, Abraham handed over a heritage to Isaac that he could carry on to the next generation. This heritage that Abraham passed on was something that his son and grandchildren could be proud to have and proud to pass on.

We must strive to pass on to our children a heritage that they can be proud of and proud to pass on. Every person deserves the right to have a proud heritage and not a heritage that they have to try to cover up. Mom and dad, don't make your children carry a heritage of shame that you have produced because of your sin. They ought not to have to carry this heritage around. Instead, live such a life that when you pass on to your reward, that your children have a heritage of which they can be proud. I am not talking about passing on money to the next generation. I am talking about passing on a life of honor, a life given to helping others and a life that was lived to give to the next generation what was given to them by previous generations. Let your children be proud to carry your name because you lived your life in such a manner that they are honored to have the heritage of your name.

43

4

Lucky or Prepared?

1 Samuel 17:50, "So David prevailed over the Philistine with a sling and with a stone, and smote the Philistine, and slew him; but there was no sword in the hand of David."

When preparation meets opportunity, the world thinks that a person is lucky. Yet in all reality I believe that this is simply the definition of success. A person who is considered lucky is most likely the person that is the most prepared. When a situation arises that calls for them to step in, they are prepared to meet that opportunity and that is why they are successful. When preparation meets opportunity and the prepared person seizes that opportunity, then they are successful. This is how championships in sports are won and this is how successful people in life become successful. Nobody is successful out of luck, for there is no such thing as luck. However, everyone that is successful is a highly prepared individual. Let me illustrate by using football as an example. A team who wins the championship is not lucky but prepared. They practice every week during the season to prepare themselves for the game that week. Then during the game, they execute the preparation skills that they practiced. Then, they go to the playoffs and practice for each game and win each game because they are prepared. Finally, by the time the Super Bowl comes, they have prepared themselves and executed the skills they practiced since spring training and they end up winning the Super Bowl, thus becoming world champions. They did not win out of pure luck! They won because they were prepared for every situation that could come their way. When the obstacles in the game came, they were prepared to meet those obstacles and that is why they won.

This is very much the case with David. Most people would say that David was a lucky man to be able to defeat Goliath, but I strongly disagree. I believe that David prepared himself and when the opportunity came, he seized that opportunity and defeated Goliath. David became successful in his life because his preparation met opportunity. David did not defeat Goliath out of luck! Let me tell you the story to explain what I am talking about.

David was out in the field watching his father's sheep when one day, according to the Bible, a lion came out and took a lamb out of the flock. David, seeing this, went out after the lion and killed the lion with his own hands. Then some days later, again while watching the sheep, a bear came and took a lamb out of the flock. David went after the bear and killed that bear with his own hands. Now David could have used every excuse in the world that he was no match for these animals, but he knew this was his duty. He prepared himself for the day this would happen by practicing with his sling; that is why he defeated them.

One day David's dad sent a messenger. He wanted him to go to the battlefield, see how his brothers were doing in the battle and carry a gift basket to them in order to help them with their needs. As David arrived at the battlefield, a huge man by the name of Goliath stepped out and began to curse the name of God. Now you must understand that Goliath was nine feet nine inches tall and his armor weighed around one hundred eighty pounds. He was one huge man! Yet as he defied God, David rose up and went after Goliath to kill him. We know the story of how Goliath mocked David and cursed David's God, yet David did not let this stop him. Even when King Saul tried to stop David, he told King Saul the stories about the lion and the bear and he said the same God who helped him defeat these animals would help him defeat Goliath. As he went after Goliath, he picked up five smooth stones, put four of them in his pocket and ran toward Goliath. Using his sling, he threw one of the stones at him, and the stone hit Goliath in the head and knocked him down. David ran over, took Goliath's sword and killed him. What a story! Most of us would say that David was pretty lucky, yet I say that David was very prepared.

If you are going to be as successful in life as David was, then I would advise that you take the same steps towards success that he took and follow them. Let me show you what made David successful.

1. He was not lazy.

In **1 Samuel 17:20** it says that **"...David rose up early in the morning..."** David was a success because he knew how to work hard. Do not kid yourself into thinking that David was a soft little boy who did not know how to work. No, the opposite is true! Taking care of those sheep everyday was a hard task. He had to feed them, water them and even defend those sheep everyday. David knew the value of hard work and his work ethic was part of the reason he became successful.

Nobody ever becomes successful without having a good work ethic. Work is not a dirty word! We live in a generation today of people who know nothing about working hard and then we wonder why we go nowhere in life. Successful people are people who work hard. Sweating and getting bloody knuckles has never hurt anyone. If we want our children to be successful in life then we had better start showing them how to work hard. You will never rise in position without having a good work ethic.

Not only did David know how to work hard but David also knew the importance of rising early in the morning. I cannot stress enough the importance of people learning to rise early in the morning. I am an early-morning person. I get out of bed every morning at 5 in the morning no matter what time I go to bed. I have learned that by rising early in the morning I can get much more accomplished in the day than I can by getting up later in the morning. You see, at the time I rise every morning, you are not going to get phone calls from people and you will not have to worry about anything taking your attention from your work. I promise you that I get more work done during the first few hours of the morning than most people do all day because I rise early in the morning. Successful people rise early in the morning. I know there is always an exception to the rule, but on the majority scale, you will find those who are successful in life are people who rise early every morning. My good friend Dr. Russell Anderson rises every morning around 4:30 and he has done this for years. Maybe this is one reason why he has run seven successful businesses in his lifetime and still has time to walk with God. He knows the value of rising early in the morning. God does not give us daylight to waste; He gives us daylight to work. You will never be successful in life being a lazy person who knows nothing about working hard and rising early.

2. He took care of his responsibilities.

Notice the phrase in **1 Samuel 17:20, "and left the sheep with a keeper..."** David knew the importance of taking care of his responsibilities in life. He was not hoping that someone else would do what he was supposed to do. It was David's responsibility to take care of his father's sheep. When his father told him to go and see how his brothers were faring in the battle, he knew it was still his responsibility to take care of those sheep and make sure they were not in danger. He left the sheep with a keeper because he was taking care of his responsibilities.

A successful person always makes sure his duties are fulfilled one way or the other. People who are successful in life do not expect others to cover for them; they cover for themselves. They realize that when they are given a responsibility that responsibility is theirs to care for even when they are gone. They do not pass the buck onto the next guy hoping that he will take care of it.

If you are going to be successful in life then you must learn to take care of your responsibilities. If you have a job to do at the church and you go on vacation, do not leave without making sure that your duties will be covered by someone else when you are gone. Successful people know the importance of taking the pressure off of their leaders by fulfilling their responsibilities. When your leaders do not have to worry about your job being done, then you will find that you are the first one to come to their mind when it comes time to promote someone to a higher position. Learn to take care of your responsibilities and stop looking for ways to get out of them. Look for ways to make sure they are accomplished. If only God's people can get this attribute, they will find themselves rising to the top in their employment and even in life.

3. He followed authority.

Again you will see in **1 Samuel 17:20** that it says that David went and did **"as Jesse had commanded him..."** David knew the value of following the authorities who were over him. We do not see him complaining about having to go and see how his brothers were doing, and we do not see him dragging his feet while obeying his father. We see him obeying what his father asked him to do.

Successful people learn early in life that if they are going to be successful, they must first of all learn how to follow authority. How in the world can you be a good authority if you cannot follow authority when you are at the bottom? You will only be as good of an authority as you have followed authority when you were under authority. If you cannot follow authority now, then you should never expect to be a good authority. If you cannot follow the authority of your parents when you are a child or a teenager then you will be a poor authority when you become a parent. Following authority does not make you a weak person, but instead, the opposite is true. When you follow authority, you are showing your strength and capability of leading. America needs a good dose of people who get back to following authority instead of questioning authority. I could not care less how the news media has drilled our society that we must be our own person and question authority. This is anti-Bible and this ideology comes straight from Satan himself. This is exactly what Satan did in Heaven before this world was ever created. He questioned God's authority and did not follow God's authority. The key to being a good authority, as even David seemed to understand, is learning to follow the authorities who God has placed in our lives.

4. He did what he was supposed to do even when others were not around.

Notice in **1 Samuel 17:34-35** that David did what he was supposed to do even when nobody was there to watch him. When David killed the lion and bear, there was no one there except for God to see him do right. David very easily could have let the lion and bear kill the sheep that they had taken and never said anything to his dad. He could have come up with a very good excuse of why this happened, but David realized he was to take care of his daddy's sheep whether his dad was there or not. It was this very thing that propelled David to the throne of Israel. You see, if David would have never killed the lion and the bear then he would have never persuaded King Saul to let him fight Goliath. Without fighting Goliath, he would have never made it to the throne of Israel. It was the paw of the lion and the bear that led to the head of Goliath which propelled him to the throne of Israel. Without taking care of the lion and the bear when no one else was around, he would have never made it to the throne. He did not know that his decision was so important, but God did. He was watching to see how David handled himself when he was alone.

If you are going to be successful in life then you had better learn how to take care of your private life. It matters not how you look on stage in front of everyone; it only matters what you do when you are all alone. You are only as good of a Christian as you are in private. You show me someone who

49

does wrong in private, and I will show you someone who one day will be caught. What do you watch on the television when you are all alone? What sites do you go to on the internet when you are all alone? What music do you listen to when you are all alone? What thoughts do you allow to go through your mind? You see, it is your private life that truly dictates what your public life will become. Those who realize the importance of doing right when they are all alone are those who will become successful in life, for God rewards those who do right when they are alone, for this is their true character.

5. He had a game plan.

In **1 Samuel 17:29,** David asked the question, **"Is there not a cause?"** David had a plan of how to defeat the giant. This is certainly what helped him become successful in killing Goliath.

Successful people are people who not only have plans for their life, but they also work those plans. A person who has no plans in life is a person who is sure to go nowhere. If you want to be successful in life then you had better learn to get some plans for your life. Teenager, life is not going to just fall into place if you have no plans for your life. Right now, as a teenager, you need to start getting some plans for your life. What do you plan on doing with your life once you graduate from school? Adults, you likewise need to have plans for your life of what you are going to do in every aspect of your life. Without plans, you will most definitely never succeed. People who are successful in life are people who make plans and have plans for what they want to do with their lives. They implement these plans so that they can succeed in these areas of their lives. You will never be successful in any endeavor of life without having plans to guide you and some plans that will motivate you when times get tough.

6. He was not intimidated by what others said about him.

In **1 Samuel 17:28-29**, David is facing the accusations that are coming from his older brother, but David did not let these accusations intimidate him. Again in **1 Samuel 17:43-44**, Goliath began to mock him and make fun of him, but David never let these things intimidate him, for he knew what and who he truly was. If David was always worried about what others thought about him then David would have never accomplished in his life what he did.

You will never become successful when all you are concerned with is what others think about you. You must realize that when rising to the top, you will get criticized. Not everyone will understand and agree with everything that you do, but you cannot let the intimidation of others stop you from doing what you are supposed to do.

For as long as I have traveled in evangelism and for as many years as I have preached, which at the time of this writing is 24 years, if I would have allowed what people said about me affect me then I would not be still preaching the Word of God. Just because someone says something good about me does not change who I know I truly am. Likewise, when someone says something ill about me and criticizes me, that does not change who I truly am. You cannot let the intimidation of others stop you, for you know who you truly are. What others say about you does not change who you are unless you yield to their intimidation. The only way they will become right is by you backing off from what you are doing and then you prove that what they have said is true. Always remember that if you are going to be successful, criticism and intimidation will come. You must not let what others say about you affect who you truly are.

7. He remembered from where his success came.

When Goliath began to talk about what he was going to do to David, David responded in **1 Samuel 17:45** that God was the source of his success and that he would defeat him because God was on his side. David knew and realized that all of his successes in life had come from God.

When you start moving up in life, and when success starts coming your way, may I remind you to never forget from where your success came. It came from God. Do not stop serving God because you are becoming successful, but keep doing what made you successful and it will most certainly keep you successful. It is always hard to stay successful the way you became successful, but if you are going to continue being successful, you must do what made you successful. When you start moving up the ladder on the job, do not let the job keep you from going to church because your faithfulness to church is part of what made you successful. When you start rising to the top of popularity because of your success, do not forget that God is the One who has promoted you to the top. God can take you down just as quickly as He put you up. If you do not believe me, then look at Job in the Bible. When success comes your way then you must realize that your success came from God, for all success in life comes from God. Do not start becoming self-reliant thinking that you are the one who made yourself successful. God will share His glory with no one. As soon as you start becoming haughty in your spirit, thinking you made yourself successful, then you can rest assured that your fall is just around the corner. You may have become successful in life, but if you are going to stay successful then you must never forget from where your success came.

8. He was not afraid to stand and fight for right.

In **1 Samuel 17:26**, we see that David was not afraid to stand and fight for right even if it meant that he must lose his life. Do not kid yourself in thinking that David did not have fears about dying when he went to fight against Goliath! David had the same feelings that every human would have had, but he realized that fighting for right was worth fighting for and worth dying for if need be.

Anyone who is going to be successful must never be afraid to stand and fight for right. Successful people do not let the fear of the consequences of fighting for right stop them from doing what is right. In life there are many things for which we can fight, but the only thing that is truly worth fighting for is truth and right. We must never cower away from fighting for truth and right. Yes, we may die and we may even lose in this fight, but we must not let the fear of losing and the fear of dying stop us from doing that which is right. In our marriages and in our churches, we can most certainly find things and people to fight, but the only thing that is worth fighting for is truth and right. In my marriage, my wife and I can certainly find many preferences over which we could fight, but over these preferences, it is not worth fighting. Now if one day she decides to stop going to church, stop serving God and even to take our daughter away from these things, then I would fight with her over this because this would be over truth and right. Oh, how we need people who will learn to fight for the right things and not be afraid to stand and fight for truth and right. Most successful people become successful because they learn the value of fighting for that which is true and that which is right.

9. He did not put things off for a better time.

Notice in **1 Samuel 17:48** that the Bible says that David **"...ran toward the army to meet the Philistine."** David did not just say that he would take care of this thing tomorrow; no, he took care of this problem immediately.

Successful people do not procrastinate! When they see something that needs to be taken care of, they do it immediately. They realize the best time to take care of something that needs their attention is right now.

My mom used to say to me, "Allen, why put off till tomorrow that which you could do today?" Oh, how right she was! Tomorrows never come, and if I wait till tomorrow then I will

53

never do that which I need to care for today. In addition to this, if I do take care of today's problems tomorrow then I cannot take care of tomorrow's problems when they need to be dealt with. The best time to take care of things is right now. If you are going to be successful in life then you must learn not to procrastinate. You must learn to take care of your responsibilities right now.

10. He was a friend to his friends.

The one characteristic that many people remember about David was his friendship to Jonathan. He and Jonathan had made a promise to each other to be friends and to always look out for each other, and they both honored this promise. David, though, honored this even when Jonathan was dead. David realized that his responsibility to his friend did not die when Jonathan died. However, his responsibility to Jonathan was to be carried out until the day of his own death.

A true friend will always be a friend. The Bible says in **Proverbs 17:17, "A friend loveth at all times..."** Once a friend, always a friend! Successful people always remember who their friends are. They will remember those who were their friends when they were nobody and are still their friends now that they are somebody. They do not let their position or success in life stop them from being a friend to their friends.

Yes, we need to be like David in being a friend to our friends. We must never let anything stop us from our responsibility of being a friend to our friends. Those who helped you when nobody else would help should never be forgotten. Those who help you when they get nothing in return are your true friends. May we also remember that though they die, this does not relinquish our responsibilities to our friends. If our friends have asked us to do something when they were alive, then even though they are dead, we should still honor our friendship with them.

11. He lived above board.

Notice **1 Samuel 18:5** where it says that David **"behaved himself wisely..."** This is teaching us that David held himself to higher standards than he held others to. He realized that as a leader he could not live where his followers lived, but he must live above where they lived, for this is what gave him the right to lead.

All leaders must learn this if they are to be successful. You, as a leader, cannot live where you expect your followers to live; instead you must live above where they live or else you lose your right to lead. Now I am not saying that you should think that you are better than they. I am saying that you cannot live on the same plane or the same level as your followers live on, for when you do, they have no reason to follow your leadership. When you are living above where they live and have higher standards and accomplishments than they do, this gives you the right to lead them and gives them a reason to follow you.

This is where most parents fail in their leadership with their children. They expect their children to be exactly like them, and hopefully one day, they will be where you are right now, but if you are on the same level as your children then they have no reason to follow you. As a parent, you must hold yourself to higher standards than you expect of your children. You must do more than you expect of your children because this is what gives them the desire to follow you. If you want your children to continue following you when they become adults, you must continue to step up in every area. The day that they arrive at your level is the day you forfeit your right to lead them. This truth applies to all leadership, whether it is on the job, in the church or in any other realm of leadership. In order for leadership to be successful at leading, then leadership must live above board, hold themselves to a higher standard and do more than they expect of their followers so that they never lose the right to lead them.

12. He had a right perspective of himself.

Last of all, as I look at the life of David, I see that David kept the right perspective of himself and never thought higher of himself than what he truly was. In **1 Samuel 18:18**, David always remembered that he was a shepherd boy. Even when he became a king, he never forgot who he truly was.

This is most certainly a great characteristic of people who have been successful for a long period of time. They never forgot who they truly were! You see, though success has come your way this does not and should not change who you are. The reason why you are successful is because of who you were. Throughout my life, I have had the opportunity to preach to thousands of people at one sitting. Every time I am done preaching to these types of crowds, I always remember the first time I had the opportunity to preach when I was a fifteen-year-old young man. I remind myself that I am still that person only with greater blessings. Just because I become successful does not mean that I should think of myself higher than I truly am. Great people and successful people learn to keep the right perspective of themselves and never let success change their outlook of who they truly are. Oh, how careful we must be to not allow success to change us.

David was truly successful in his life and his success was not just by mere chance or luck. His success in life came from living these principles that we have just learned. If we want to become successful in life then we should mimic the principles that made David successful.

5

The King Maker

1 Samuel 10:1, "Then Samuel took a vial of oil, and poured it upon his head, and kissed him, and said, Is it not because the LORD hath anointed thee to be captain over his inheritance?"

1 Samuel 16:13, "Then Samuel took the horn of oil, and anointed him in the midst of his brethren: and the Spirit of the LORD came upon David from that day forward. So Samuel rose up, and went to Ramah."

When looking at the life of Samuel, maybe nothing encourages me more than to realize that Israel had Samuel because of a godly mother. Never underestimate the importance of having a godly mother or being a godly mother. We know the story of Hannah. She was brokenhearted because of her desire to have a son, and yet, for some reason which she did not understand, God had closed her womb and had not allowed her to have a child. She became so broken over the matter that she went to the temple to pour her heart out to God and to ask for a child. Eli the priest, seeing her pray and thinking she was drunk because he only saw her lips moving, told her to put away her wine and strong drink. Yet Hannah told Eli it was not that she was drunk but that she was pouring her heart out to God asking for a son. Eli told her that within a year she would have a son. Eli's prophecy came true when Hannah conceived and brought forth her first child Samuel. The amazing thing about this story was that she had promised God to give her son back to Him if He would give her a son. She kept her promise by giving Samuel back to God and allowing Eli the priest to rear him.

Without this godly mother who prayed for a son and then gave him back to God, Israel would have been without a prophet whose legacy became that of a king maker.

In his lifetime, Samuel anointed two kings, and honestly, was responsible for preparing Israel for these kings. There is one thing for certain, every nation needs a Samuel: a man who from childhood to death lived right and became a king maker. A man who would take boys and make kings out of them. Without king makers like Samuel, nations will crumble and God's people will go aimlessly into deeper sin because of a lack of leadership that will lead them the right way. What we need are people who will take up the mantle of a Samuel and determine to be king makers like Samuel was. Let me show you the characteristics of the man who was a king maker and what made him to become the person and king maker that he was.

1. He started serving God as a child.

In **1 Samuel 3:1** it says, **"And the child Samuel ministered unto the LORD before Eli."** Samuel did not wait until he was an adult to start serving God; he started serving God as a child. Not only did he start serving God as a child, but we also know from studying his life, that he was a very godly young man who lived a right life in spite of the pressures of others around him who were not living right.

Let me say, you are never too young to serve God. It matters not what your age is; if you are old enough to get saved, then you are old enough to start serving God. You do not have to wait to be an adult to serve God. No! Even as a child you can start serving God. I believe the best time to start serving God as a soul winner is when you are a child. The first person I ever led to Christ was when I was at the age of seven. I can remember my aunt, Bessie Parr, taking me out to the park to go soul winning and training me to be a soul winner. I can remember her teaching me the importance of witnessing to even my friends with whom I would play. So, the next day while I was playing with my best friend, I asked him if he was saved and he had no idea what being saved was. So, I took a New Testament that my Aunt Bessie had given to me and showed him how to be saved. That afternoon he bowed his head and trusted Christ as Saviour. Thank God that my Aunt did not think that being seven years of age was too young to be a soul winner. Since that time I have literally led thousands of people to Christ all because as a child my Aunt showed me the importance of being a soul winner. Yes, Mom and Dad, you ought to teach your children to be soul winners and don't let them wait until they are adults to start serving God. Teach them as children to be soul winners. The boldest soul winners you will find will be those people who were trained to go soul winning as a child.

We must not let age be an excuse to not serve God. We must get our children, like Samuel, to start serving God at a very young age. Listen, it would be better to serve God as a child and have no regrets than to live in the world and regret those years you wasted that you could have used for God.

2. As a child, he served the man of God.

Notice again in **1 Samuel 3:1** that Samuel ministered not just to the Lord, but he also ministered unto Eli. You see Eli was his preacher, his man of God. Part of the making of a king maker was that he was taught the importance of the position of the man of God.

The best way to keep your children out of trouble is to push them to be around the man of God. I will guarantee that if your children spend time with the man of God, they will be less likely to mess up their lives in sin, because most people who are around the man of God are much more careful about what they do. The man of God represents God, and they don't want to do wrong around him.

Your children will serve the man of God if mom and dad will teach them the importance of the position of the man of God.

For instance, when I was a child, I was never allowed to call the man of God by his first name. I could call him "Brother so-and-so or Preacher or Pastor", but I was never to call him by his first name. If I ever thought about doing that, I promise you, I would have had a bar of soap in my mouth faster than you could blink an eye. My parents taught me that the man of God's position was an honorable position. They taught me to respect him by addressing the preacher in the right way. They taught me to serve the man of God by finding out things that he liked, like candy bars, and then we would go to the store and buy the preacher his favorite candy bar and give it to him. What were my parents teaching me? The importance of the man of God! If children are taught this early then they will carry it through life.

Another way they would teach me the importance of the preacher's position is by not allowing us to talk bad in our house about the preacher. That was something that could get us into some serious trouble. Parents, if you are going to turn your children out to be king makers, then they must be taught the importance of the position that the man of God holds. That means you MUST NOT talk bad about the preacher in your house! When you start talking bad about the preacher, you are tearing down his position to your children and you will ultimately cause your children to never want to become a king maker. Samuel served the man of God because he had parents who taught him that this position was very important. When a child sees the position is important, he will want to serve the Lord and the man of God.

3. He listened to and obeyed his preacher.

We have the story in **1 Samuel 3:5-9** about God calling Samuel while he was in his bed at nighttime. We see that the first time when God called Samuel, he immediately ran to Eli the preacher and asked him what he wanted. Eli said he had not called. This happened a second time and then again a third time. At the third time Eli realized that it was God trying to talk to Samuel. Now Eli told Samuel that the next time he heard the voice that was calling him, he was to say, **"Speak, Lord; for thy servant heareth."** Samuel did exactly what the preacher told him to do! Why did he do this? He was listening to the preacher. By listening to the preacher, he could then obey the preacher. Do not underestimate the importance of Samuel listening to Eli, for this was part of what made Samuel the man he was and the king maker he became.

Our children need to be taught to listen to the man of God and also to obey the man of God. They need to be taught not to question what the preacher tells them to do but to obey the preacher when he preaches to them and tells them what to do personally. We need to teach our children, like Samuel was taught, to not ignore the preacher and put him off. We need to teach our children that when the preacher speaks, we listen and obey.

How do we do this? Well, we teach our children to listen to the preacher by making them listen when he is preaching in church. We ought not to let our children draw pictures while the preaching is going on or sleep while the preacher is preaching. No! Make your children sit up and listen to the preacher as he preaches. I can remember as a boy sitting by my mom in church and how she made me listen as the preacher would preach. I was the type of boy that when I sat down and was still for any length of time, I would fall asleep. Well this would not happen in church or else my mother would pinch the inside of my leg and make me stay awake while the preaching was going on. What a shame that in our society we allow our children to do their homework during the preaching time and let them draw pictures while the preacher is preaching. You are teaching your children not to listen and obey the man of God. I also believe you should not let your children run to the restroom while the preacher is preaching. Is it not amazing how your children can sit for hours and watch television and play video games and never use the restroom; however, when the preacher gets up to preach, they all of a sudden need to go to the restroom? Parents, make

61

your children go to the restroom before the services. This will teach them the importance of listening to the preacher as he preaches.

I also believe you need to teach children the importance of listening to the preacher and obeying him by going to him for counsel. One way that I do this is when my daughter Caitlyn comes to me for advice, every once in awhile, I will act as if I don't know the answer and I will tell her she needs to ask the preacher about this question. I will take her to the preacher and tell her to ask the preacher what she should do, even though I know what the preacher is going to tell her what to do. What am I accomplishing by doing this? I am teaching her that one day when she becomes a teenager and even an adult, she can run to the preacher at any time for advice, listen to him and obey what he counsels her to do. We as parents would be wise to teach our children the importance of listening to the preacher and obeying him by taking them to him for counsel even though we already know what the answer is. This is all part of turning our children out to be king makers.

4. He was open to the call of God.

I need not have you read it again, but in **1 Samuel 3** we read the story of God calling Samuel to be the future prophet of Israel. As a child Samuel was so close to God that he could hear the voice of God when God called him. As a child he realized that the calling of God was the highest calling that a person could have. He was not so busy running around with his friends that he could not hear the call of God. He did not let his personal desires squelch out the calling of God. Samuel was open to the call of God and this is why God used him and not other young men of his age.

Young people need to be taught the importance of surrendering to the call of God. Every preacher and every parent should make the call of God very important and big. I say to every preacher and parent, do not just be satisfied with your children serving God, raise the standard high and let your children know that you want them to serve God full time with their lives. I get tired of people saying that as long as their children are serving God then they will be happy. I understand what they are saying, but the truth of the matter is, our children can only rise as high as the lowest standard we have set for them. If we tell them we will be happy with them if they will just serve God then that is all that they will go after because that is the lowest standard we have set for them. What we ought to do is raise the standard and tell our children we want them to serve God full time in His service. I know what I am saying will make some preachers and parents upset, but it is about time that, instead of lowering the standard of expectations for our children, we raise the standard of expectation for our children. They will rise to whatever we expect of them, because they are followers. By nature, if children have a good relationship with their parents and preacher, they will want to meet the expectations that their leaders have for them. My parents did this for me, and I thank God that they told me time and time again that they hoped one day I would become a preacher. I imagine if they would have lowered the standard of expectation for me then maybe today I would not be a preacher. Oh the importance of being open to the call of God, for God cannot use you to be a king maker if you are not open to His call.

5. He made the Word of God important in his life.

Notice in **1 Samuel 3:19**, it says that Samuel, **"let none of his words fall to the ground."** These words were the words of God. Samuel at a young age made the Word of God an important part of his life. He listened to every word and soaked it up like a desert soaks up rain. He listened intently to the words of God and made sure that he was not missing one of those words that God had spoken to him. When did all of this happen? It happened when he was a child! As a child he made God's Word important and I believe this is one of the key ingredients to becoming the king maker that he was.

63

Every child should be taught the importance of the Word of God. We should teach them that they need to listen intently to the Word of God and let nothing slip by so that they do not miss one of God's words. Do not ever expect God to use you to make kings if you do not make His Word important and spend time with the One who makes ordinary people into kings. God can never show you that one He wants you to help become a king if you do not make the Word of God important in your life.

There are a few things that I was taught as a child that helped me to understand the importance of the Word of God. First of all, I was taught to never set anything on top of the Bible. I know this seems petty to most people, but this is what my parents taught me because they wanted me to understand the importance of the Bible. To this day I never set anything on top of the Bible, because I feel that the Bible is the most important Book in the entire world. My parents taught me the importance of treating the Bible right and always knowing where my Bible was. I think every child should be taught the same. This is what makes the Word of God important to our children. Secondly, as a child my parents taught me that I was not to have a bite of food until I had spent time in the Bible. Now I can understand right now as people are reading this that many may think my parents were being cruel to me, but the truth is, they were teaching me the importance of the Word of God. They were teaching me that the Bible was more important to our living than having food to eat. Now I know eating food is important, but it did not hurt me to read some Bible before I ate any food in the morning. King makers must make the Word of God important to them if they are going to make kings. Samuel did not allow any of God's words fall to the ground because he felt that God's words were precious and important, and they are!

6. He was a man of his word.

You read in **1 Samuel 9:6** that Samuel was **"an honourable man."** The word "honourable" means that he was a man of

64

his word. He took his word seriously. When he told someone he was going to do something, he did it. Notice that this was not Samuel saying that he was honourable; it was the people of the city saying that he was honourable. When people say this about you, then you know that your word can be trusted.

God will never use a person who cannot keep their word. Keeping your word is a sign of character, and having character is part of making kings out of boys. How can you train someone to become a good king if you cannot keep your own word? There is no way that you can do this without being a person who keeps your word, and maybe this is why you struggle in making kings out of boys. King makers must be people of character: people who honor their word.

In the society that we live in today, it is no wonder we have a lack of leadership because we have a lack of people who will keep their word. You can sign contracts and get out of those contracts if you have a good attorney. You can tell someone something and then try to say that you really did not mean it the way that it came out. Our society lacks good leaders because it lacks people who honor their word. If you say you are going to do something, then do it! Find a way to do it because you gave your word and your word is something you should never just let slip by.

7. He never lost his walk with God.

Notice in **1 Samuel 9:15** that Samuel, on the day before, had heard God speak to him in his ears. What was this? This was Samuel still having a walk with God even after he had been serving God for many years. Though he had risen to prominence in society and though he had served God for many years, he never lost the importance of having a daily, personal time with God.

You must never get to the point in your life when you feel you do not need to spend as much time with God as you used to. We must realize that no matter how long we have served

God, we still need God just as much today as we did when we did not know as much about God. In fact, if the truth be told, the more you do for God, the more you need to walk with God. How can we expect to do the work of God properly if we do not spend time with the God whom we are serving? The longer you teach a Sunday school class, run a bus route to pick up children or serve in some capacity in the church, the more you need to walk with God. We should never lose the importance of walking with God! When you get too busy to walk with God then you are too busy! Whenever you rise to a position where you think you do not need to walk with God anymore, then you have risen too high for your own good. We must understand that the more we do for God, the more we must spend time with Him so we can get the instructions we need to do His work.

King makers never lose their walk with God. Your walk with God today should be sweeter and more precious than it was the first time you walked with God. Samuel realized this in his life and still took time out of his busy schedule everyday to walk with God. Whether you are a preacher or even a lay person in the church, you must never lose the importance of having a walk with God, for this is what keeps you in tune with making kings.

8. He was concerned with how people treated God.

I bring you to the story in **1 Samuel 8:6** when the people came to Samuel and demanded of Samuel to give them a king. This demand bothered Samuel not because they were refusing him, but because they were refusing God's leadership over them. Samuel was a man who was concerned with the treatment of God. I can think of one other person in the Bible who was like this, and that was King David. Maybe David picked up this trait from Samuel. I do not know, but I do know that Samuel was displeased that the people were treating God this way.

King makers must be a people who are concerned with the treatment of God. Like Samuel, king makers should not make themselves the issue, but they should make God the issue in life. It ought to bother us when God is being mistreated in our society. It ought to bother us that God was kicked out of our public school system by kicking out prayer and the Bible, and yet, our school system will embrace humanism. It should bother us when the Ten Commandments are kicked out of our court systems because they are kicking God out of our judicial system and our society. We need a people who once again get bothered when God's name is used as a curse word and when God is literally pushed out of society for the sake of political correctness. King makers are concerned with the treatment of God. Are you?

9. He felt preaching truth was more important than political correctness.

You can figure out how I feel about our politically correct society. I look at **1 Samuel 15:12-26** and read the story of Samuel coming to King Saul to rebuke him for his sin of not totally destroying the Amalekites. When Samuel came and preached this sermon to King Saul, we must understand that Samuel was putting his life on the line for preaching truth. He did not have his finger up in the air testing which way the wind was blowing to decide what to say to King Saul because it was popular at that time or because it is was non-offensive. No, Samuel preached exactly what God had laid on his heart without counting the consequences of what may happen to him. He felt that obeying God and preaching what God told him to preach was more important that being politically correct.

If we are going to have king makers once again in our society, then we must get away from worrying about whether something is politically correct. We must preach and teach that which is scripturally correct. This is how you make kings and this is how you turn boys into kings. If all you do is count the consequence of the battle instead of counting the

67

consequence of not preaching the truth, then you will never become the king maker that you are supposed to be. King makers must be concerned and consumed with truth more than they are concerned and consumed with being accepted by society. You check out the past generations that in their lifetime and ministries saw many people surrender to serve God, and see if they were concerned with what people thought about them or if they were concerned with what God thought about them. Oh, how we need a generation again of people who become consumed with truth and not political correctness, so that we once again may turn out a generation of young people who will become kings in their own ministries and serve God for the rest of their lives.

10. He had a right attitude concerning the fallen.

I want you to notice in **1 Samuel 15:35** the attitude of Samuel after seeing King Saul fall into sin. He did not rejoice over the falling of a man, but instead it bothered him and the Bible says that he **"mourned"** for Saul. He was not happy that he was right about what he told Saul; though he was right. Instead it broke his heart that a man of God had fallen from the ranks of doing right.

King makers never rejoice when someone has fallen or when someone has compromised. You may have seen it coming and you may have even said this was going to happen, but if you are going to be a king maker, it should literally break your heart when people mess up their lives or when people fall away from the truths that they had been taught by others. In my lifetime I have seen many a great person fall into sin, and I will be quite honest with you: the longer I live, the more it breaks my heart that people mess up their lives in sin. I never rejoice when I hear of a ministry that has strayed from the old-time religion. The truth is that my heart breaks when I hear of good men and good ministries that are changing from what they used to be. I am compelled to mourn and pray for these more than I ever have before.

King makers should never be thrilled when they hear the news of someone falling, for we don't need less people in the ministry. We need more people in the ministry. If you are truly going to be a king maker, then you must carry the same attitude of Samuel when hearing of the fallen: it should break your heart!

11. He never let failures stop his vision of being a king maker.

Notice in **1 Samuel 16:1** how God rebukes Samuel from mourning over the life of a fallen king, and God tells him, **"fill thine horn with oil, and go…"** Once Samuel picked himself off of the ground after seeing King Saul fall, he grabbed the horn that he used to anoint kings and went back out to anoint another king. Though someone in the past whom he had anointed had failed, he did not let that stop him from going back out to make another king out of a boy.

If you are going to be a king maker, then you will have to realize that you will have casualties of those whom you have made into kings. When this happens, you cannot let this stop you from helping another to become a king. If all you do is mourn over your failures, then you will never make another king.

I wonder how many people have quit trying to anoint another king just because one in the past has fallen. They get that attitude of, "Is it really worth it?" If Samuel would not have picked up his horn, then we may never have read the story of David and Goliath. If Samuel would not have picked up his horn, then maybe Israel would have never experienced the great man of God that David was. You just never know whom you are hurting by dwelling on the past failures of those who have fallen in your ministry. If you do not become like Samuel and pick up your horn and go after others, you may be missing a "David" of whom you could make into a king. What a tragedy this would be that you would miss the greatest blessing of your ministry all because you dwelled on the past failures of your ministry. King makers must have tough skin and realize that there will be casualties. You cannot allow the casualties to stop you from pursuing others that you can turn into kings.

12. He knew that character was more important than stature.

One of the things that made Samuel the king maker that he was, is that he learned the importance of looking at the heart of the person and not at the stature or talent of the person. In **1 Samuel 16:7** we see Samuel being taught by God not to look at the stature of an individual or the talent of an individual but to look at the heart and see what God sees.

When making kings, we must realize that it matters not what a person's talent is, and it matters not what their stature is or whom they know in life. The most important thing in making kings is what is in the heart of the individual. This is why we must not make the mistake of seeing how much talent a person has, because talent without character equals disaster. You give me a person with little talent but with much character, and I will show you a person who will go pretty far in life. Do not fall trap to looking at the stature or talent of someone in deciding whether you want to invest your time in that individual to try to help them become a king. Instead, look at their heart and see if they are sincere, have character, and if they are, then invest in that person. King makers must learn that character is far more important than stature.

As I close this chapter, let me just say that Samuel, even when he died, continued to minister. At the death of King Saul, God allowed Samuel to come back for one final message to the old king. King makers can be assured of one thing: though they may die, a king maker's ministry will still go on and their voice will still speak though they be in Heaven. I think of my mother who has recently gone to Heaven. She had a big impact in the forming of my character, which has made me into the man of God I am today. Though I am not a great man of God, my mom's voice will continue to speak until the day I die because I will continue to tell the stories of what she had done for me and through me, as you can see in this chapter. My mom lived her life to be a king maker and her voice will continue to speak though she is in Heaven. If you want the same, then invest your life into the making of kings and queens out of boys and girls in your church, and your legacy and voice will live on even though you will be in Heaven.

6

Good Beginnings Don't Guarantee Good Endings

1 Samuel 9:2, "And he had a son, whose name was Saul, a choice young man, and a goodly: and there was not among the children of Israel a goodlier person than he: from his shoulders and upward he was higher than any of the people."

1 Samuel 15:26, "And Samuel said unto Saul, I will not return with thee: for thou hast rejected the word of the LORD, and the LORD hath rejected thee from being king over Israel."

Have you ever read a book that was great at the beginning but when you got to the end of that book, the ending was not as good as the beginning? How disappointing it is when the ending of a book does not match or even get better than the beginning. It is almost as if you feel that you have wasted all of your time reading this book because the end did not match the beginning. As people we are always looking for a better ending because that is really the way God made us. When something starts out with so much promise and then ends in such a disappointing way, we feel that we have been cheated of the time we invested in reading.

No story in the entire Bible represents this illustration more than the life of King Saul. Saul's life started out with so much promise and ended with so much regret and disappointment. It is almost as if the life of Saul comes in a two-part book. If you were to read the first part of Saul's life and then read the second part of his life without knowing that it was the same person, you would think that you were reading about two separate people. What a promising start Saul had in his life! He was a young man whom God describes by saying there was not a "goodlier person" than he. When God looked over the whole nation of Israel, He could not find one person who was a better person than Saul. Saul, in God's eyes, was the best person in the whole nation of Israel and this is why God chose him to be the first king of Israel. Yet, when you look at the last part of his life, what a tragic story! Here is a man, who at the end of his life, was powerless, bitter and vengeful to the point that he even tried to kill his own son-in-law. It is a tragedy that a life could start out with so much promise and talent and end in such a tragic way. Yet the whole change in his life can be narrowed down to one incident.

God had told Saul to go and completely destroy all of the Amalekites for the wickedness that they had done to Israel when they left Egypt. God said that He wanted everything destroyed; every person, every animal and anything that was breathing was to be destroyed. Saul and the people thought they knew better than God. When they went to war, they destroyed everything but the best of the flocks and the king of Amalek, King Agag. They said they wanted to keep the best so they could make a sacrifice to God. The problem was that this was not what God had commanded. It matters not what good you want to do with your disobedience: it is still disobedience. Because Saul would not accept that he had done wrong, God pulled His blessing away from Saul and left him.

You see, we are all one incident away from turning the good beginning of our life into a bad and tragic ending. It does not matter what your position is or even what you have done for God in the past, every one of us is one decision or one incident away from ruining our life. As we look at the life of Saul, we see a waste of so much potential. Let me, over the next few pages, show you the difference between the good beginning and the bad ending of his life. Let me divide his life into two parts and show you what made him the "goodlier person" and then the steps that led to his tragic ending.

Part 1 – The Making Of A "Goodlier Person"

1. He was obedient.

It is amazing to me that this is one of the qualities that seems to pop up in many of the great people in the Bible. God honors obedience! In **1 Samuel 9:3-4** we have the story of Saul's father, Kish, telling Saul to go and seek the asses that had been lost. Apparently their herd of donkeys must have become loose and now Kish needed someone to go and find them. As he tells Saul to go, you will notice that Saul did not question his father and did not delay in obeying his father. Saul went immediately, which truthfully is what obedience is all about.

Obedience is certainly a big thing in the eyes of God. God honors those who learn to obey. When a person learns to obey, then God knows that they can be trusted. You are not being obedient when you are told to do something that you were going to do anyway. The reason this is not obedience is because it took no effort on your part because you were going to do it anyway. True obedience is when you are commanded to do something that you were not going to do, and yet you do it and do it immediately. Obedience is something that is done without delay. When you are commanded to do something and then delay in doing it, you are being disobedient.

The truth is that obedience is something that anyone can do. You don't need talent to be obedient. You don't need strength to be obedient. You don't need intellect to be obedient. The only thing it takes to be obedient is simply to do what you have been told. It is amazing that even an animal can be obedient to their master. Now if an animal can be obedient I would think that a human, and especially a Christian, can be obedient. This world needs a revival of obedience among God's people. When God chooses to use someone, you had better believe that God is going to choose someone who knows how to obey.

2. He listened to the man of God.

We come back to the same story about Saul looking for the herd of animals that his father had sent him after. Notice in **1 Samuel 9:18-22** we see that the prophet Samuel commands Saul to go with him to perform a sacrifice. Now this is when Saul was going to be anointed king of Israel by the prophet Samuel. We see that Saul trusted in the man of God, listened and did what the man of God told him to do. He followed his word to the letter. You must understand that at this time Saul hadn't found the herd of asses that were lost, and yet, at the commandment of the preacher, he listened to what the preacher told him to do and did it.

Yes, it is important for us to acquire this attribute in our life. Though I have dealt with this subject in another chapter of this book, let me just reinforce this point one more time. Oh, how important it is for us to not only be present where the man of God is but to also listen to what the man of God says to do. Many people today are present in church and are present in the preacher's office when he is giving counsel, but the truth is that they are not actually listening to what he is saying. There is nothing more frustrating as a preacher than to preach something on Sunday morning and people go right out and do the complete opposite of what was just preached. Or when you preach something and then the very next day someone asks you for advice about what they should do, yet it was just preached about the day before. Now listen, I am all for going to the preacher for advice and being in church for the preaching time, but don't just be present in body. Be present with your ears and mind. Pay attention and listen to what the preacher is saying. We could be helped so much more if we would not only be present, but also actually listen to what is being said by the preacher!

On top of all of this, let me say that if we are going to listen to the man of God then we need to be in church to hear him speak. Most of the time the preacher speaks through his preaching. If we are not there to hear him preach, how can we listen to him? We must learn the importance of being in church every time the doors are opened, for we never know which service is going to be the service when the preacher will say something that will change our life. When God looks for someone to use, you can guarantee that God is going to look for someone who listens to the man of God.

3. He had a right perception of himself.

I love this part of Saul's life! Samuel had just told Saul that he was going to be the next king of Israel. When Saul hears this, he responds by saying, **"...Am not I a Benjamite, of the smallest of the tribes of Israel? and my family the least of all the families of the tribe of Benjamin? wherefore then speakest thou so to me?" (1 Samuel 9:21).** Now here is a man who had a good perception of himself. He wondered what there was in him that God would even want to use. This was not the response of a person with low self-esteem, but this was the response of a person who had a proper perception of himself. He realized it was an honor that God even wanted to use him.

You will never excel in serving God when you have the wrong perception of yourself. God uses people who have the right perception of themselves. For instance, we should never think that we are better than someone else or that we are any worse than anyone else. Having the right perception of ourselves comes from realizing that God knows what our strengths and weaknesses are, and we must look at ourselves through the eyes of God. When we do this, we will have the proper perception of ourselves. In every pursuit of life that we are going after, we must keep ourselves in proper perception. We must know what our strengths are and even what are weaknesses are. We must not think that life owes us everything, but we also cannot think that we are sub-human and worthless. If God made us, then we are at least the creation of God and that makes us someone of value. However, on our own merit, we are nothing. It is only through God and His grace that we can ever do anything. Until we get the proper perception of ourselves, we will always be holding ourselves back from what we could be and do for God.

4. He received his desires from God.

As Saul now is leaving Samuel to go back home after being anointed king, you will see in **1 Samuel 10:9** that **"God gave him another heart..."** What was this other heart? God placed His desires inside the heart of Saul. Saul was no longer running off of his own personal agenda or desires; he was now pursuing the desires that God had placed in his life.

When you lay aside your desires for the purpose of fulfilling God's desires, this is most certainly one of the most important keys to becoming a "goodlier person" in the eyes of God. What is even better is when you no longer have to lay your desires aside to do God's desires because your desires have become like God's desires. The only way this can happen is for God to place His desires in you. You say, how can I get this to happen? God tells us how this can happen in **Psalm 37:4**, **"Delight thyself also in the LORD; and he shall give thee the desires of thine heart."** God says that the way to get Him to give you His desires is to delight in Him.

Now how would I delight in God? Let me explain this by using something that I delight in very much. I love chocolate-chip cookies! Now when I say that I love chocolate-chip cookies, that is saying it lightly. I like the type of cookies that are pulled out just a little before they are done to allow them to be gooey on the inside. When my wife, Sandy, makes me chocolate-chip cookies, I love getting them when they are still hot and soft. I get three or four or however many I can get my hands on, and I start biting down on those cookies enjoying and savoring every bite. What am I doing? I am delighting myself in chocolate-chip cookies by eating them and enjoying each bite.

This is exactly what God wants of us if He is going to place His desires in us. When we start delighting in God by reading

His Word and when we start delighting in Him by spending time praying everyday, and finally when we start delighting in Him by serving Him, God starts to take our desires out of our heart and replaces them with His desires. You see, whatever you spend the most time thinking on and doing is what your heart will desire to do. You get God's desires by spending time with Him, and this will cause you to start having the same desires as God. When a person starts to have the same desires that God has, he can be guaranteed that God will be pleased and this person will be considered a "goodlier" person in the eyes of God.

5. He was a Spirit-filled man.

Notice now that Saul had left the prophet of God to go back home. **1 Samuel 10:10** says that **"...the Spirit of God came upon him..."** No wonder he had God's power upon him! Any person who has the desires of God will most likely obtain the power of God to fulfill these desires. Saul did not get this power by pursuing his own desires. He received the Spirit of God upon him by getting God's desires in his heart and then going out to do what those desires dictated that he should do.

Any person who is going to be used of God in a great way is going to have to get God's Holy Spirit power upon them. I can tell you how to start to get this power, go out and delight yourself in God until God starts placing His desires in you. You will be surprised how much easier it will be to get His Holy Spirit to fill you. It takes God's power to fulfill His desires. Most certainly God noticed this in Saul's life and I believe this was one of the reasons God called him a "goodlier" person.

6. He was a humble man.

Now look at **1 Samuel 10:16** where it says, **"...of the matter of the kingdom, whereof Samuel spake, he told him not."** This was nothing more than humility of heart. This was a man who was not bragging about who he had become or what position he had acquired, but instead he just went about his business as usual.

This is what humility truly is. Humility is not walking around with your head hanging down as if you are trying to prove that you are humble. Truly humble people won't have to tell others that they are humble. Humility is truthfully just going after the responsibilities of life as you usually go after them without having to tell everyone about the position that you just received or the power that you just acquired. Humility is not about you or your position; humility is simply having the proper state of mind about yourself and the responsibilities that you are required to do. When a person receives a higher position, that doesn't mean they should change the way they do things. They should go about doing things the way they have always done them. That is what humility truly is. You see, the way up is never to promote yourself. The way up is to do what you are supposed to do with the proper mindset. God uses people who are humble and keep themselves and their positions in the right perspective.

7. He never sought position.

One of the great things about the early part of the life of Saul was that he never sought to get position. In fact, we see the opposite is true in **1 Samuel 10:22**. He avoided trying to get position. When the people came to make him king, the Bible says that **"…he hid himself among the stuff."** Saul, in the early part of his life, was only interested in doing his job and obeying. He was not trying to get the best position for himself.

How different this mindset is from today's mindset. We live in a generation that says if you want position then you must seek that position. May I say, any position acquired this way is only going to reveal your weakness as a leader. Great leaders don't seek position. Great leaders seek to do their duties and people make them leaders. When God saw this quality in the life of Saul, God knew this was good. Likewise, if we are going to be used of God we cannot seek position. God does not place people in His higher positions because they seek them. God finds those who are busy doing His will for their lives and God promotes those who are already doing that for which the position calls. Yes, good people will NEVER seek position; only selfish people will seek position.

8. He ignored the criticisms of man.

Like Saul, a good person cannot be concerned with the criticism of men; they can only be concerned with doing right. When people started to criticize Saul in **1 Samuel 10:27**, Saul responded to their criticisms by not responding: **"…he held his peace."** This is a sign of good people, and even great people. When criticism comes, they learn not to listen and respond to the criticism. Saul realized that if he were to respond to what they had said, he would be lowering himself to what they were. Just because they said these things about him did not change what he truly was.

We must learn that when criticism comes our way, the best way to respond to it is to have no response at all. Most of the time our character will respond for us! If we live a life of character and people begin to criticize us, our character will reveal the fallacies of their criticisms. You see, most of the time our critics just want to get us to respond in some way. We ought not give them the pleasure of knowing that they got us to respond. When you respond by criticizing back then you have become no better than the critic. Oh, the importance of people learning that the best response to criticism is no response at all. Let us simply let our character defend us and be our response to the critics.

9. He had a purpose in leading.

This is one of the reasons Saul was such a good man. When Saul became the leader, he had a purpose in leading. His purpose in leading was revealed in **1 Samuel 11:7**, and this purpose was to defend God and truth.

Every good person who has position must realize that when they lead, they need a purpose in leading. That purpose should be to get those who follow them to do what is right. This is what God saw and wanted in Saul; a purpose in leading His people. Whatever you lead, make sure you have a purpose in why you lead those who follow you. Whether you lead in the home, on the job, in the church or even in society, you must have a purpose in leading other than to say you are the leader. Good people will follow leaders who have a purpose in leading. The purpose is not about the leader but about truth and right.

Part 2 – The Fall OF A "Goodlier Person"

Now as we come to this point in Saul's life, we see some things begin to change. This is what led Saul to have a bad ending. I have shown you what made Saul a "goodlier" person, but now let me show you the steps that led him to his bad ending, so that we can avoid the same steps and the same results.

1. He became enamored with his position and power.

One of the first things you see in the steps that led to Saul's demise is that he began to place his eyes on himself and think that he was something more than what he truly was. In **1 Samuel 13:11**, we learn that Saul was concerned with what the people thought about him. He was more interested in holding onto his position than he was about doing what God had told him to do. He was so concerned about losing his position that he was willing to disobey the commandments of God.

How dangerous this type of mentality is for a person who holds any type of position. When you become more concerned with holding your position than you are with doing right, then you have some serious problems. If I must lose my position for the sake of doing right, then I must be willing to lose that position. Listen, position is not worth having if you

81

have to lose your character to keep that position. This is certainly one of the main problems in the political spectrum of today. People will do anything to get elected even if it means they must compromise what they believe in order to get that position or keep that position. Position is never more important than right and wrong. We must realize that when we become more enamored with our position than with truth, we are headed down a bad path.

Not only was Saul enamored with what people thought about him, but Saul also got a "big head." When Samuel was rebuking Saul in **1 Samuel 15:17**, he said to him, **"...When thou wast little in thine own sight..."** As long as Saul didn't think he was a "big shot" Saul did fine, but when the day came that he became so enamored with his position and thought he was "someone", this is when we see Saul make some very foolish decisions.

We cannot let the position we have risen to go to our head. As long as Saul was humble God used him, but the very second that Saul began to think he was somebody and became more concerned with his position than doing what was right, this was when he began to fall. Whatever you do, always keep yourself little in your own sight. Realize that no matter to what position you have risen, you have that position because of God and not because of who you are. Don't let position cause you to get too big for your own britches, because, if you are not careful, you will split them britches, and that can be mighty embarrassing. Eating crow is never fun. The best way to keep yourself from having to eat crow and keep yourself from splitting your britches is to stay little in your own sight. Don't get enamored with your position.

2. He made compromise a part of his life.

I will promise you one thing: nothing good comes from compromise. We see in **1 Samuel 14:21** that Saul started to allow the people to mingle with the Philistines, and this is nothing more than compromise. As a leader he should have stopped this immediately, but instead he simply let it go on.

If you want to head down the road of destroying your life then go ahead and compromise what you have practiced and taught all of these years. Time and space would not allow me to tell you how many good people I have seen destroy their lives and ministries all because of that one word called "compromise." Let me just say this about compromise – **A PERSON NEVER EARNS THE RIGHT TO COMPROMISE**. I do not care what accomplishments you have mad in life, compromise is always wrong no matter who does it. I recall great men of the past who got older and compromised. They were doing things that they used to preach against, and some simply covered their eyes to this compromise and said that they have earned the right to do this. NO! You NEVER earn the right to do wrong! Show me in the Bible where God says a person has earned the right to do wrong. Wrong is wrong no matter how you put it and no matter who does it. If God judged David for his wrong after all that he had done for God, then why do we think that we are better than David and that we have earned the right to compromise and do wrong? If something was wrong when you were younger then it is still wrong today even after all of your accomplishments. I have become so weary of this mentality because we are telling a younger generation that compromise is not bad if you have earned the right to compromise. If it is wrong for a young person to do something then it is also wrong for an older person who has accomplished a lot to do the same thing. Right and wrong is not right or wrong because of what we have accomplished. Right and wrong is right or wrong because it is either right or wrong. Let us always remember that we never earn the right to compromise, and compromise will always lead us down a path that will eventually hurt us. Is it not amazing that the very people with whom Saul allowed his people to compromise were the very people who ended up killing him? That is exactly what compromise will do!

3. He took his eyes off of God.

I need not spend much time on this point as I have already talked much about this at an earlier point in this chapter. Let me just point out that in **1 Samuel 15:11** Saul had turned his back on God. That means if he turned his back on God then he was only facing one person, and that was himself.

Any time you take your eyes off of God you are only going to place them on one person, and that is you. This is simply a life of selfishness, and, may I say, selfishness will never satisfy. Don't think that you can spend your life living for you and be happy. No! You live a happy life when you spend your life living for God and keeping your eyes on Him.

4. He stopped following all of God's commandments.

In **1 Samuel 15:11**, God said that Saul had not performed His commandments, and yet in **1 Samuel 15:13**, Saul said he had **"...performed the commandment of the Lord."** Now if I had to choose between trusting God's Word and trusting Saul's word, I believe I would be wise in trusting the One Who has never lied. Saul's problem was that he was trying to pick and choose what part of God's commandment he wanted to follow and that is why he said he had followed God's commandment.

Let me just say that anything but following all of God's commandments is nothing more than disobedience. Partial obedience is not obedience at all! We cannot just say that we will follow the part of God's Word that we want to follow and then throw the rest away and think we have done right. This is one of the biggest problems in our society and in our churches today. We want to pick and choose what commandments of God we want to do, and if we don't want to do it then we say that we don't have to. Now it does not matter how you try to justify this in your mind so that you can live with yourself; anything short of following all of God's Word and commandments is nothing but disobedience. When we

84

come to the point when we only follow a portion of the commandments of God, and this portion is what we want to do, then rest assured that heartache is soon to come, for God cannot and will not bless partial obedience to His Word. It is like a person thinking they have tithed because they gave 5% of their income when God commands you to give 10%, for this is what a tithe is. Anything less than 10% is truthfully no different than not giving at all. I mean, if you gave nothing at all, this would be the same as giving 5% of your income and saying that you tithed. Likewise, anything short of following all of the commandments of God is just like not doing it at all and it is disobedience.

5. He was only sorry for being caught in his sin and not for committing the sin.

What a tragedy when a person comes to the point in their life when they are only sorry for being caught and not for the wrong that they have done. In **1 Samuel 15:30** Saul was not sorry because he had sinned; he was sorry because he was caught. This is the difference between King David and King Saul. They both did wrong, but one was sorry for being caught and the other was sorry that they had done wrong. When we get to the point when we think this way, our final destruction is not far off.

Let me ask you several questions: Are you sorry that you lied about something, or are you sorry that you got caught in the lie? Are you sorry that you got caught breaking the law, or are you sorry that you broke the law? Are you sorry that you got caught in your adultery, or are you sorry that you committed adultery? I could go on and on naming sin after sin, but the point is that the difference between those who can turn their lives around and those who won't is whether or not you are sorry about your sin or are you only sorry that you got caught? A changed life can only happen because of repentance, and repentance only comes when a person is sorry they have done wrong. I can not stress this point enough, but a person who is never sorry for their wrong and is only sorry for being caught will continue to do the wrong once the authority is gone. One of Saul's final mistakes was that he never was sorry for his wrong, and because of this, he never got right with God and ended his life as a bitter man.

6. He made life evolve around him.

We see the final story of Saul in **1 Samuel 28:15**; right before his death, we see him breaking a law that he had made all for the sake of pleasing himself. At this point his whole life revolved around himself.

A sure sign of a person who is backslidden and away from God is that life must revolve around them. Everyone must do what they want and everything must be what they want. This is nothing more than being backslidden. If you want to find out whether you are backslidden or not, then look at the past few days of your life; is everything that you do about others or is it about you? Is your perception of others dependant upon how they treat you and what they think of you? Is your perception of situations based upon what you think of them and not what God thinks of them? When all of life must revolve around you, then you are backslidden! If your marriage must revolve around your desires, then you are backslidden. If your job must revolve around what you want, then you are backslidden. If your family must do everything that you want, then you are backslidden! If your church must do everything that you want to keep you happy and faithful to church, then you are backslidden! We are not the issue in life; truth is the issue. When we make ourselves the issue in life, this is nothing more than being backslidden.

In closing let me say, our goal in life ought to be to make the ending of our life better than the beginning. God never intended for our ending to be worse than the beginning. If you want to avoid making your ending worse than your beginning, then avoid what made Saul's ending so tragic and bad. Instead, follow what made his beginning so bright and promising.

7

A Burden for Souls

Romans 9:3, "For I could wish that myself were accursed from Christ for my brethren, my kinsmen according to the flesh:"

I don't know if there is anyone other than Jesus Christ that exemplified their burden for souls more than the Apostle Paul. We see in this verse his burden for souls was so great that he was willing to bear the curse of sin upon himself and go to Hell if needs be, just so that people could get saved. What a man, what an example, what a life, what a Christian the Apostle Paul was that he would carry such a burden for the souls of men.

There is maybe no human to whom the Gentile world owes more of a debt than to the Apostle Paul. It was Paul whom God used to pen the majority of the New Testament. It was Paul whom God used to bring the Gospel to the majority of the Gentile world. Probably the greatest reason he did this was because of his burden for the souls of mankind. It was his burden for souls that drove him to live the life that he lived. When you look at where he came from, it is no wonder that he had such a burden for souls.

Paul from his birth was a Pharisee, as he explains in **Acts 23:6**. We know the Apostle Paul from the beginning of his life as Saul, as this is the name that was given to him from his parents. Saul, when he came of age, practiced the Jewish religion as a Pharisee in the strictest of definitions. He was very adamant that everyone should serve God the way that he did. Yet there was a deacon in the church by the name of Stephen, whom Saul was standing by and watching as Stephen was stoned to death for preaching the Gospel of

Jesus Christ. Saul became so zealous in this practice of religion that he gave his life to have those executed who practiced any other way than what he was taught. One day as he was walking down the road to Damascus, the Bible says he saw a bright light and a voice spoke to him and said, **"...I am Jesus whom thou persecutest: it is hard for thee to kick against the pricks" (Acts 9:5).** Jesus Himself witnessed to Saul. Saul was under such great conviction about his need of the Saviour that he tried to cover it up by killing the saints of God. At this moment, we see that Saul accepted Christ as his personal Saviour. Immediately Saul got involved in the church and became a soul winner and started to lead people to Christ, just like any Christian ought to do. As time went on, people began to call him Paul instead of Saul, as this is the name by whom most of us know him. Paul later on was ordained and went out as a missionary to start churches all over the known world of that day. No doubt the Apostle Paul is responsible for us Gentiles receiving the Gospel as he gave his life to see souls saved.

No wonder Paul had such a burden for souls! He had seen and experienced how people could be so stooped in religion that they are blinded to the simplicity of the Gospel. Paul saw this in his life and had given the remainder of his life, after being saved, to show people the truth of salvation. What a debt we owe to this great man. I don't know, but maybe the greatest way that we could pay back this debt to him is to get the same burden for souls that the Apostle Paul had, so that we would also become ardent soul winners for Christ. Oh, how we need more Apostle Paul's in every region of the world so that this world can be reached with the Gospel. How churches need to get a burden for souls like Paul had as thousands, yea, millions of people around them are going to Hell. Someone must reach these people with the Gospel. As we study the life of the Apostle Paul, maybe we will acquire the same burden for souls that he had. Let me show you just a few of the qualities that helped make up this great man. Please understand that there is no way that we could give justice to the Apostle Paul in one chapter, but as I show you some of his qualities, you can copy what he has done so that we can reach our world for Christ.

1. He realized God could use him in spite of his background.

As Paul describes himself to the church of Corinth in **1 Corinthians 15:9** he says, **"For I am the least of the apostles, that am not meet to be called an apostle, because I persecuted the church of God."** Paul knew what he had done before he got saved and he realized how wicked his life was as he went around persecuting the church and even executing Christians. He knew in all reality that he had murdered many Christians and that he was not worthy to even be called an Apostle. Yet he also knew all of this was under the blood of Jesus Christ, and though he did not deserve to be called an Apostle, he was not going to let his background stop him from being a soul winner and serving God.

Let me say to those who read these pages and come from a less than desirable background, there is no sin that the blood of Christ cannot cover. Because of this you must realize there is no background that would disqualify you from being a soul winner. It matters not how deep you were in sin, for the blood of Christ is what has reached down to you to save you from that sin. It is this same blood that is going to save others who are in the depths of sin. We must be the ones to bring the Gospel to them so they too can be saved. You cannot let your background stop you from being a soul winner. It matters not if you are a convict who has a criminal record, God can still use you to be a soul winner. It matters not if you were a thief or a robber, God can still use you to be a soul winner. It matters not if you have killed people and are known as a murderer, God can still use you to be a soul winner. It matters not if you are a pedophile, prostitute, or any other wicked sin that we could name, God can still use you to be a soul winner. Listen, God knew what He was getting when He saved you from your sins. If God did not want to use you to be a soul winner, then He would not have saved you. But He did want you just like you are, and He did save you. Now He wants to use you to be a soul winner for Him.

As long as you let your background hinder you from serving God, or from being a soul winner, then you are limiting what God can and could do through you. For God to use us despite what our background is only testifies of the power of God and what His power can do for people. Use your background to show the world the power of Christ in your life and the power of the blood of Jesus and what it can do for people. No, we don't have to brag about our past sins, but we can show people what Jesus' blood can do for anyone no matter how deep they are in sin. Never let your background be the excuse that keeps you from being a soul winner.

2. He did not let his education make him too good to win souls.

We learn in **Acts 22:3** that Paul received his education from Gamaliel, one of the greatest doctors of law of his time. Gamaliel was a respected educator and a well-known educator of his day. Paul received his education from this man. We should realize that Paul was a very educated man and was not some ignorant person who did not know anything about education and especially the law. Paul was very educated, yet he did not let his education stop him from being a soul winner. He realized that being an educated person did not make him any better than anyone else. He realized that being educated did not give him a license to sit at home and never tell anyone of the Gospel of Christ. Paul realized that there was no excuse for not being a soul winner, including his education.

It does not matter how much education you have in life, you are never too good to be a soul winner. Just because you are well educated and may be a pretty brilliant person, this does not excuse you from winning souls to Christ. The Bible commands everyone that is saved to be a soul winner. Whether they are uneducated or educated, they are to be a soul winner. We should not think that soul winning is just for the ignorant and unlearned. No, soul winning is the command of God for everyone. Paul never let his education stand in the way of being a soul winner.

I think of a good friend of mine, Dr. Wendell Evans, who was involved in education for many years, and for the majority of his life was the president of Hyles-Anderson College. Here is a man who knows history like no other man, and he is a well-educated man, yet you will find him every week out trying to win souls to Christ. I think of another friend of mine, Dr. Jim Jorgensen, who himself is a very educated man and has been involved in education his entire adult life. If you were to go to Kentucky and visit him on the weekends, you will find him visiting children on bus routes so they can be brought to church on Sunday. You will find him on Saturday's out knocking on doors trying to lead people to Christ. These men are very well educated men, yet they realize that their education does not give them an excuse to sit at home and not win souls to Christ. Instead, they, like Paul, understood that the command to win souls is to everyone. I say to those who are well educated people, you are to be a soul winner just like the Apostle Paul was. Your education does not make you too good to win souls to Jesus Christ.

3. He did not let his lack of proper speech stop him from winning souls.

We learn in **2 Corinthian 11:6** that Paul says he was **"…rude in speech…"** Paul, though an educated man, was not the best orator as he himself describes his oratory skills. Though he was not good at public speaking, he still did not let this stop him from winning souls to Jesus Christ. Again he realized that his inability to speak properly was not an excuse to not be a soul winner.

We should always realize that though we are not the best speakers we are still commanded to be soul winners and win souls to Christ. God knew when he commanded you to be a

91

soul winner what your speaking skills would be, and still He commands you to be a soul winner. Why? Because God realizes that it is not how well we speak that determines whether a person can get saved, it is the power of the Holy Spirit of God working in the heart of a person that causes them to get saved. God can take the well-refined speech and use it to convict the souls of men for their need of a Saviour. But God can also use the rude, choppy delivery of the plan of salvation to convict the souls of men. I am always amazed when I take people soul winning how God uses people to win souls to him. I have heard people witness, and I will stand there thinking to myself that there is no way this person will ever get saved out of such a delivery. Then in a few minutes I see my lack of faith in God's power reproved as a person bows their head and receives Christ as Saviour. You see, it is not in the eloquence of the delivery that determines whether a person gets saved, it is in the power of the Holy Spirit convicting lives that a person gets saved. God just needs voices to deliver the plan of salvation to a lost and dying world. Without voices people will die and go to Hell because they never accepted Christ as their Saviour because they never heard this message. God uses people, whether they are eloquent or not, to deliver his plan of salvation to the lost world. This is why we must not let our lack of eloquent speech stop us from winning souls.

4. His burden for souls was greater than his desire for pleasure.

In **Romans 9:3** we learn about the Apostle Paul that his desire to see people saved was more than a responsibility, it was his burden and it was his life. Paul became so burdened for the souls of men that he wished, if it were possible, for him to be cursed so that others could be saved. Paul had such a great burden for the souls of men that this burden for souls became his life and his whole reason for living.

The day when you get past going soul winning because you have to, and instead you go soul winning because people go to Hell and you don't want them to go there, is the day when you will start seeing lives changed. Soul winning ought to be more than just a responsibility that we have to do every week to appease our conscience that we are doing right. Soul winning ought to become our life so that no matter where we are and no matter what day it is, we are conscious of those around us and the eternity that they will spend either in Heaven or Hell. Soul winning should become such a part of our life that we witness to people because we just don't want them to go to Hell. Now don't get me wrong, if the only reason why you go soul winning is because you are supposed to go, then you keep going soul winning because you are supposed to go. Don't you stop soul winning just because you don't have the burden for souls that you ought to have and because soul winning is not your life. Yet, when soul winning becomes a lifestyle and is something that you do everywhere you go because you care for the souls of men, then you will no doubt start seeing great results in those to whom you witness.

I recall awhile back I was out soul winning on a cold winter night. As I knocked on a door, a lady came to the door and answered and allowed me to talk to her for awhile. I went through the plan of salvation and got down to the point where I asked her if she would be willing to pray and receive Christ as her Saviour. She looked at me and asked me if she could ask me a question. She asked me what I got out of this if she got saved. My response was that I didn't get anything out of this other than to see her in Heaven some day. She looked at me somewhat startled and said to me, "You mean the only reason why you are here at my door telling me how to go to Heaven in this cold weather is because you care about me?" To this response I said, "Yes." Tears began to run down her face as she said she had never seen anyone care for her in such a manner, and within a couple of minutes she prayed and received Christ as Saviour. Oh, the importance of God's people getting to the point in their lives when they just want to see people saved, and they go soul winning, not out of obligation, but out of a genuine love for the souls of mankind.

93

5. He realized the hope of changing the world was the Gospel of Christ.

Paul realized the only hope of this world being changed was for people to get saved. He realized the only way he would ever change the world was to get more people saved and the more people that got saved the more change he would see in this world.

How messed up we are in this day. We try everything else to solve the problems of this world other than that which will truly change this world. I watch Christians get caught up in things that are not bad things thinking these will change their country, and yet they don't realize that the hope to stop the problems of this world is to get people saved. Look in the book of Acts and see how they turned the world upside down for Christ. It was through going out and winning people to Christ and starting churches everywhere. Listen, the hope of this nation or any nation is not politics. The way to stop all the social problems we have in this world is not through secular organizations. Though I am not against these organizations and I think many of these organizations have done some good in society, the only thing that will truly change this world is to change people. The only way you are going to change people is to get people saved. The only way they will get saved is if someone will be a soul winner and bring the Gospel to them. The way to stop abortion in our society is to lead the doctors who perform these abortions and young ladies who would have these abortions to Christ and show them the right way to live. The only way we are going to stop the gang problems, drug problems, crime rate, pornography problems, and any social or sin problem we have is to get people saved, into church and under the preaching of the Word of God. Soul winning and starting churches is the answer for this world. It worked in the book of Acts and it will still work today.

6. He refused to let circumstances dictate his attitude.

In **Acts 26:2** the Apostle Paul is standing before Agrippa making his defense for his life as apparently Agrippa must have asked Paul why he was so happy. Paul responds to Agrippa in this verse by saying, **"I think myself happy..."** Though Paul was in prison, he never let the chains that bound him and the coldness of the prison cell take away his joy and happiness. He told us how he kept himself happy, which was that he thought himself happy. He was saying that instead of letting circumstances dictate whether or not he would be happy, he chose what to think on and this is how he became happy. He would not let the chains think for him; he would think for the chains. He would not let the cold prison cell think for him; he would think for the prison cell. He realized there was something inside of him that gave him a reason to be happy, and this reason was salvation.

As long as you let daily circumstances decide whether or not you are going to be happy, you will be miserable and unhappy. The day when you decide to think for yourself and start thinking about what Christ did for you on Calvary is the day when you take control of your happiness. This then becomes the day when you can think yourself to happiness. You need not let your health think for you; you should think for your health. You should not let your finances think for you; you should think for yourself. You should not let the adverse circumstances of life think for you, instead, why don't you think for those adverse circumstances and be happy in life despite these circumstances? If you are saved and on your way to Heaven, you have a reason to be happy and you have a reason to be joyful. When you start thinking about your salvation and realize that there is nothing that can take this away, then you can be happy in life in spite of all the bad circumstances that may have come your way. If you can start thinking yourself to happiness, like Paul did, then you can become a better soul winner, for when you are joyful in spite of circumstances, you can be a better soul winner for Christ.

7. He was not afraid to work to pay his bills.

In **Acts 26:3** you will read that Paul had to stop for awhile to earn some money to keep on going so that he could continue to win souls to Christ. He did not let his lack of finances stop him from being a soul winner. Instead he went out and started making some tents to earn some money so he could continue to win souls to Christ and do what God had called him to do.

How important this is for full-time servants of God to realize that, if needs be, they get a job to pay the bills so that they can still do what God has called them to do. We are no better than the Apostle Paul, and if the ministry cannot pay our way, then we should find a way to keep the ministry going, but don't ever stop being a soul winner.

8. He used his infirmities as a means to minister.

You read in **2 Corinthians 12:9** that Paul had prayed for God to remove some sickness that he had. Three times Paul asked God to remove this sickness and three times God told Paul that His grace was sufficient to help him through this sickness. Then, we read in **Galatians 4:13**, **"Ye know how through infirmity of the flesh I preached the gospel unto you at the first."** What we learn about Paul was that he did not let this sickness stop him from being a soul winner or a preacher. Instead what we learn is that Paul used this sickness as a means to minister to those with whom he came in contact. He realized that if God did not see fit to remove the sickness, then apparently God felt he should use this sickness as a ministry to serve God.

Let me say to those who carry infirmities, sickness or even trials in your life, if you have prayed for God to remove this infirmity from you and God has not removed it from you, then apparently God has given it to you so that you can use it for His glory and as a ministry to minister to others who are going through the same thing. Always use the trials that you face in life as a means to minister and help others. Always use these trials to witness to those who are lost who are going through the same trials that you are or have gone through. I am reminded of a teacher of mine in college, Mrs. Marlene Evans, who for nineteen years fought cancer and used that cancer to minister to others. Instead of letting the cancer destroy her, she decided to use that cancer as a ministry to encourage others, and that she did. Let us never waste the opportunities of soul winning and ministry that God sends in our lives through sickness and trials. Let us use these infirmities in our lives as a means to witness to others. Maybe the reason why God sends these things our way is so that we will become a better soul winner for Him. I know not why they have come, but instead of letting these things afflict you, why not use them to minister to the needs of others?

9. He realized God's power is given in the trials.

Notice again in **2 Corinthians 12:9** what Paul says about his trials, **"Most gladly therefore will I rather glory in my infirmities, that the power of Christ may rest upon me."** Notice that Paul realized that God's power came upon him through the trials of his life. This is why he could glory in these trials. It was through the trials that he received God's power.

Well, the same is true for us. You will never receive God's power on your life without trials in your life. God's power is never given on the mountain top but God's power is given in the valley. In **Psalm 23:5**, the Psalmist, as he talks about the valley, says, **"...thou anointest my head with oil..."** People who want the power of God on their lives are going to have to walk through the valley to get this power, for this is where God anoints His people with His power. Paul realized that the reason why God sent Him through the trials of life was so he could get God's power to become a better soul winner. Christian, don't run from your trials in life, instead realize that God is sending you through these trials so that He can give you His power to enable you to be a better witness for Him

97

and a better soul winner to the lost. Don't waste the time of trials that you face, instead use these times to get His power so you can be a better soul winner in order to reach more people for Him.

10. He never let persecution stop him from winning souls.

Through the end of the life of Paul we see him facing persecution for his witness of Christ, and never do we see him pulling back his message of salvation because of persecution. Instead we read in **1 Thessalonians 2:2**, **"But even after that we had suffered before, and were shamefully entreated, as ye know, at Philippi, we were bold in our God to speak unto you the gospel of God with much contention."** Paul said that even when the suffering came because of persecution, he continued preaching the Gospel and preaching it more boldly. Not only did he not let persecution stop him from winning souls and preaching the Gospel, but he also through the persecution became bolder for Christ. He loved the souls of men so much and had such a burden for these souls that he would not let persecution stop him from being a witness and a soul winner.

Let me ask you a question (though truthfully we don't know the answer until faced with persecution): What is it going to take to stop you from witnessing for Christ and being a soul winner? If you let the little bit of ridicule of others stop you from being a soul winner, most definitely you will never stand when persecution comes. We don't go soul winning because it is the popular thing to do, we go soul winning because it is a command of God and it is right to do. We don't go soul winning because it is easy; we go soul winning because there is a Hell. How amazed I am of what little things we let stop us from being soul winners. We will let the fear of being kicked off of a property stop us from witnessing to others, and what a shame if this stops us from soul winning. Let me just say, if there is a Hell, and people will go there if they don't get saved, then we should not let anything stop us from witnessing to the lost. I am not saying we should be rude and belligerent with people, but I am saying we should not let these little things stop us from witnessing for Christ. There is a Hell, and people will go to that Hell if they don't accept Christ as their Saviour from their sins. This is why we MUST witness in spite of what may come. The little persecution we receive on this earth is much less than the suffering of Hell that those who do not get saved will experience for an eternity if they don't get saved.

11. He realized the greatest fight to fight was for the souls of men.

Notice what Paul says in **1 Timothy 4:7**, **"I have fought a good fight, I have finished my course, I have kept the faith:"** Paul says that the fight for the souls of men is a good fight and he said that he fought that fight. He didn't just say that he fought a fight, but he fought a good fight. He made his fight for the souls of men a fight worth watching.

We should realize if we are going to go after the souls of men and be soul winners, then it will be a daily battle that we will fight. It is not easy and never will be easy to be a soul winner, but the fight is worthy of fighting. Listen, there are several battles that we can get involved in and fight for, but the one battle that is worthy of fighting is the fight for the souls of men. Oh, how every Christian needs to get involved in this fight and make it a good fight. Let us not just quit soul winning at the first sign of adversity or discomfort, but let us realize that the fight for the souls of men is a spiritual warfare. This spiritual warfare that you embark upon as a soul winner is the hardest type of warfare that mankind can fight, for we are not just fighting for the physical freedoms of mankind, but we are fighting for the freedom of the soul so that soul can spend an eternity in Heaven some day. We do not fight against man, but against Satan and his forces. This fight is a worthy fight, and a fight that, if you are going to be successful as a soul winner as the Apostle Paul was, you will fight for the rest of your life. Be like Paul and make this fight for the souls of men that you are in a good fight, a fight worthy of watching.

12. He never wavered in his faith.

How important this point is! Paul said in **1 Timothy 4:7**, **"...I have kept the faith..."** Paul said in his zeal to see people saved he never compromised his faith to see someone saved. He said he kept the faith to the end. The word "kept" in this verse means "to guard." Paul said he guarded his faith that he would not let his zeal to see souls save cause him to compromise this faith. He was saying that he let the faith keep his zeal in check.

One thing that you will always have to be careful of is that you don't let your zeal to see souls saved cause you to compromise the faith that you preach. In your zeal, keep your faith. You must always let the faith keep your zeal in check and let the faith decide whether or not it is right to do something. Let me explain! I can think of a well-known evangelist who several years ago stood for the old-time religion. But because of his desire to see people saved, he was willing to compromise his faith to get bigger crowds so he could see more people saved. Now the truth is this man did see more people saved, but in pursuit to see people saved he did not keep the faith. He did not let the faith keep his zeal for souls in check. I can understand wanting to see people saved, but compromising the faith to see more people saved is wrong. I would rather do right rightly and see less people saved that do right wrongly and see more people saved. I know many may disagree with me on this, but the faith that was given to us by Christ is to never be compromised. Everyone must get saved the same way and if they won't get saved without us compromising, then that is their fault and not ours. Our responsibility is to give out the Gospel without compromise; their responsibility is to receive the Gospel. Now we can't make them accept Jesus Christ as Saviour, but we can sure keep our part and never let our faith waver and defend our faith. There are many sincere people out there whom I believe truly want to see people saved, but they have compromised the faith in order to do this, and this is wrong.

Paul said he kept the faith, and we also in our zeal and burden to see people saved must keep the faith.

13. He finished what he started.

I love this about the Apostle Paul, as he says in **1 Timothy 4:7, "...I have finished my course..."** Paul said that as he came down to the end of his life that he finished what he started out to do, and that was to win souls to Christ.

Let me beg of everyone who reads this manuscript to finish what you start. They say the average Christian only serves God for seven years. This means there are many casualties in the Christian life. Don't be one of those casualties! Finish what you started to do, and that is, you started to serve God and win souls for Christ, now finish your life doing just this. If serving God is worth starting then serving God is worth finishing. If soul winning is worth starting, then soul winning is worth finishing.

How we need every Christian to be like the Apostle Paul and get a burden for souls and then use that burden as motivation to be a soul winner. Every Christian is to be a soul winner and lead souls to Christ. This is what He has left us here to do. Now let us get started in the winning of souls. To those who have started and have relaxed a bit or even quit soul winning, finish your course. The course that you are to finish is to be a soul winner until the day that you die.

8

A Foolish Wise Man

1 Kings 4:29-30, "And God gave Solomon wisdom and understanding exceeding much, and largeness of heart, even as the sand that is on the sea shore.   And Solomon's wisdom excelled the wisdom of all the children of the east country, and all the wisdom of Egypt."

Job 32:9, "Great men are not always wise: neither do the aged understand judgment."

With so much wisdom you wonder how Solomon could be so foolish. Here was a young man that virtually had everything going for him that a person could have and yet he blew it with his foolish living. Here is a young man that had a very good father, had wisdom given to him from God, had the respect of the people that were following him, had more money than anyone that was alive in that day, and even had God's blessings upon him as he started his kingship, and yet when you come to the end of his life you see someone who pretty much wasted everything that was given to him by his parents and God. Let me explain by briefly telling you the story of his life.

Solomon was the youngest of all of the children of King David. He was the youngest in his family, with his older brother being Adonijah. On top of this, his family was the result of an adulterous affair between David and Bathsheba. As he grew up, he had seen his half brother Absalom rebel against his dad and try to steal the kingdom from David. He saw how God stepped in and destroyed Absalom and brought the kingdom back to David. He saw how his big brother Adonijah had   taken   the   throne   illegitimately   by   declaring himself king. And yet I am sure that Solomon wondered about this as the kingdom was promised to him by his father, his preacher, and God. Yet again, God steps in and takes Adonijah out of the throne and sets Solomon on the throne through the help of Nathan the prophet and his mother Bathsheba. Now Solomon is the king of Israel and God comes to him and offers him a blank check to ask God for anything that he wanted from God and God said He would give it to him. Solomon, being humbled by the fact that he was even the king of God's people, asked God to give him wisdom and understanding, and God did just that, plus added to him riches and honor. He starts his kingdom by pursuing the desire of his father David, by building a temple for the people to worship God. Solomon was successful in all of this and even became the wealthiest man in the world during his lifetime. Yet, with everything that God had given to Solomon and with what he had seen God do through him and for him, he still lived his life foolishly. Let me explain! Solomon, instead of marrying one of his own people, married seven hundred women, all from other nations. Nowhere in the Bible do we know of Solomon having a wife from his own people, the Israelites, as God had commanded His people to do. Not only had he done this but he also had tried to find pleasure in "things" and not in God. At the conclusion of his life, he realizes how much of his life he had wasted, as read in the book of Ecclesiastes.

In the book of Job, the young man Elihu was right when he said, **"Great men are not always wise..."** What a shame that Solomon wasted so much wisdom by living such a foolish life. There are several lessons that I believe we can learn from the life of Solomon that will help us to not waste any of the wisdom that God has given to us.

1. Background does not have to determine your destiny.

Let me remind you that Solomon was the youngest of King David's children, and in these days it was custom for the oldest child to take over the inheritance of the father. This would mean that by custom Solomon had no right to the throne of Israel. On top of this, Solomon was the result of an affair. Let me put it plainly, he was in all reality an illegitimate child! If anybody could say that their background was going to hold them back from doing anything great in life Solomon could have said that.

We must understand that background has never and will never determine a person's destiny in life if they choose to not use their background as a crutch for failure. Tell Moses who was a murderer that background matters! Tell Gideon who was a scared farmer that background matters! How about the Apostle Paul who was a mass murderer, tell him that background matters! You can go through the Bible and, the truth is, many of the people that God used in the Bible had backgrounds that were not the greatest. Yet the reason why God could use them is because they didn't let their background become a crutch that they could lean on for failure.

May I say to anyone reading this book whose background is less than desirable: your background does not have to determine your destiny. You may be a child that comes from a single family home or even a dysfunctional home, but don't let this background hold you back from letting God do something great through you. Maybe you live in the ghettos somewhere and the neighborhood in which you live no one has ever done anything worthwhile in society or in life for that matter. As long as you don't let this be your crutch for failure, where you live does not have to determine your destiny. It matters not how much you have failed in the past and it matters not how ugly your past looks. We must realize that we serve a God that is powerful enough to use the background that we came out of to bring glory to His name by using us. Don't you think that God knows what your background is? Don't you think that God knew before you were even born what type of background you would have? Let me just say to you that the background of a person will only hold them back if they allow it to hold them back. I cannot express enough my feelings on this matter, that your background does not have to be the determining factor in whether or not you are going to be successful in life or not. Listen, everyone has something in their background that is less than desirable, but it is only those that do not use it as a crutch to lean on for their failure that do something with their lives. Somewhere you have to break the chains of background in your life. Determine that you will not let your background hold you back, but that you will use your background to help motivate you to excel in life and also to help others who are facing the same conditions that you have faced in your life. All we need and must understand is that the background of Solomon did not determine his destiny in life and likewise does not need to determine your destiny in life either.

2. God's timing is the best timing.

Imagine with me what must have been going through the mind of Solomon as he knew that he was supposed to be the next king of Israel once his father, David, had passed away, and then to see Absalom take the throne from him. Again, imagine with me what he must have been thinking when his older brother, Adonijah, had illegitimately taken the throne. I could imagine Solomon sitting there thinking in his mind and wondering if God was truly going to come through for him, and if He was, when was God going to finally step in and do what He said He would do? Maybe even Solomon was becoming a little impatient waiting on God, yet Solomon had to wait on God's timing to come through for him. But, while all of this was happening, we never see Solomon trying to push God's timetable ahead, and we never see him complaining to God about when God was going to do what He had promised him. Solomon simply had the patience that it takes when it comes to waiting on God's timing to come to fruition. In God's timing everything works perfectly. We see his patience in God's timing pay off in **1 Kings 2:12** when it says, **"Then sat Solomon upon the throne of David his father; and his kingdom was established greatly."** Patience in God's

105

timing always pays off because God's timing is always the best timing. His patience in God's timing paid off when this verse says that God established his kingdom greatly.

Patience is always the key for God's timing to work. We must understand that when it comes to God's timing, God does not work by our calendar or our watch. God has His own timetable and we must not find ourselves trying to rush God's timing. We must be careful about this because God just may give us what we want and then we may lose the blessings that we have right now. We need to understand that God is rarely early, He is never late, but God is always on time! God will always come through like He says He will and it takes our patience for this to happen.

When it comes to God answering our prayers, we must have patience that God, in His perfect timing, will come through. Those maybe that are waiting on God to lead them to the right person to marry must have patience in God's timing. If you rush God, He may just allow you to get exactly what you want, but it may not be whom you should marry. I can remember in my own life how I wondered if God was ever going to lead me to the one that I should marry. It was not until I was twenty-six years of age that I married my wife Sandy. For many years I had people pushing me and trying to set me up, but I just believed that God had the right person for me. With patience in Him, He led the paths of my wife and I across each other.

Oh, Christian, don't try to rush God's timing. Just have patience that no matter what the situation is, His timing is always best. His timing is best when it comes to our health! His timing is best when it comes to our finances! His timing is best when it comes to our job and the future of our jobs! His timing is best when it comes to the death of a loved one! His timing is always best, and we must trust that God's timing is best, and He knows what He is doing. Do not question His timing, but instead have patience in His timing.

3. Leadership must make decisions with their head and not their heart.

I look at the story in **1 Kings 2:13-25** when Adonijah had come to Bathsheba and asked her to ask Solomon to allow him to marry Abishag the Shunammite, who was the nurse of King David at the end of his life. Solomon, when approached with this question, was faced with a hard decision that had to be made even though it probably went against the grain of his heart. We must always remember that the people of the Bible had feelings just like we have feelings. When this was asked of him he had no choice than to have his older brother executed because his request was treason. Adonijah's whole purpose in asking this was because he wanted the kingdom to come back to him. Solomon faced a hard decision. He had to order his older brother to be executed even though his mother had asked him this question. This certainly was an early test of leadership and he passed with flying colors. He did not make the decision with his heart, but made this decision with his head.

You see, leadership must not let their heart be the decision maker. They must make decisions with their head if they want to be successful. When the heart makes decisions, the heart will base its decision on what the emotion of the moment dictates or by what will be the easiest decision for the decision maker, so as to not hurt someone they love. Yet the head makes decisions based upon what is right and what is wrong, and this is the way that leadership must make decisions. Every leader is faced daily with decisions, and if they let their heart make decisions for them, they will end up hurting themselves and those whom the decision affects.

Parents, you must make decisions concerning your children with your head and not with your heart. If you are not careful as a parent you will let up on your children because you think that they have had it too rough, and the only thing you are doing is hurting the future of that child. Any parent that is worth anything does not enjoy punishing their children, for it

107

hurts them when they have to punish them. Yet a parent must make the decision for their children with their head and punish them when they need punishing. If we don't punish them for the wrong and let them get away with the wrong because it is too hard to punish the child, then what you are teaching that child is that they can get away with doing wrong their whole life. This is just not true. If children don't know that there is pain in doing wrong, then they will continue to do wrong. Now don't get me wrong, I am not talking about beating your children, but I am talking about punishing your child the way that the Bible commands us to punish children. What will happen one day is that your child, if they never feel the pain of doing wrong, will one day break a law that requires them to face our judicial system, and may I say that the judicial system has no heart for your child. This is why you, as a parent, must not let your heart make the decisions for you concerning your children. As hard as it may be, you must make decisions for your children with your head.

Likewise, the same is true about any form of leadership. All leadership must make decisions with their head and not their heart. A business owner that runs his business from the heart and not from the head will fail. You cannot pay the bills with your heart. A pastor that makes decisions on how to run his church from his heart and not from his head will end up hurting his people. Making decisions from the heart is not just. It is not just because you will make different decisions based upon the situation. This is why a school principal and even a school teacher must make decisions concerning their students with their head and not their heart. Even the president of the United States and the judges that sit on their benches must make all decisions from the head and not the heart, for the head will make the decision based upon what is right and what is wrong. This just may be one of the hardest things for leadership to do, but it must be done. Solomon learned this early in his kingdom.

4. Wisdom, understanding, and discernment are better than riches and honor.

We read in **1 Kings 3:5-15** how God came to Solomon in the night and asked Solomon what it was that God could give him. When Solomon was faced with this great question, it did not take him long to come up with the answer. He knew what he wanted from God. He told God that all he wanted was God's wisdom and understanding to lead God's people the way that God wanted them to be led. He said in **1 Kings 3:9, "Give therefore thy servant an understanding heart to judge thy people, that I may discern between good and bad..."** What Solomon was asking of God was for God to give him wisdom, understanding, and discernment, for he knew this was the greatest asset anyone could have. He asked not for riches, fame or even honor, all he wanted was the mind of God to make the proper decisions.

May I say that this should be the prayer of every person alive! Our daily prayer to God should be for God to give us His discernment to choose between the good and the bad. Then ask for His wisdom to know how to do the good that God wants us to do, and finally ask for the understanding to know how to break down God's wisdom so that we can explain it to others so they may do the same. Everyday of my life my prayer is filled with this request for God's discernment, wisdom, and even His understanding. We must never sacrifice the discernment, wisdom, and understanding of God for the sake of riches and honor. Riches and honor will not bring happiness. If you don't believe me just look at the sports world and look at those in Hollywood who have plenty of money and extreme amounts of fame. Their lives are filled with heartache and sorrow because they have not the discernment, wisdom, and understanding of God. If we ever must choose between having riches and honor or having God's wisdom, discernment, and understanding, my advice would be to always choose the latter, for the latter will give you joy and happiness in life where riches and honor cannot give this to you.

5. The blessings of God are not inherited; they are earned.

Notice in **1 Kings 3:7** that Solomon acknowledged that he was now king in his father's stead, yet Solomon realized that God's blessings on David's life were not something that he would inherit but something that he must earn. Solomon realized that he would not naturally have the blessings of God on his life that his father had just because he was his son. Solomon acknowledged and realized that if he was going to have the same blessings that his father David had, then he must earn those blessings. This is why he asked God for His wisdom.

One of the greatest fallacies I see in our generation is that so many people think that just because someone's father was a great person that they automatically will have the same blessings on them. May I say that this is not the case. Just because God's blessing is on a preacher does not mean that God's blessing will be on his children. His children must earn those blessings the same way their dad earned those blessings. I watch preachers all over the country put their children on their staff and everyone immediately thinks that their children are going to do the same things that their dad has done in the ministry, and this is just not true. Now don't get me wrong, I am not saying that a pastor should not hire his children, what I am saying is that his children must earn the blessings of God the same way that their dad earned God's blessings.

Let me even go one step further in explaining this point. To those who are children of preachers, you are not spiritual just because mom and dad are spiritual. Now I am a preacher's kid, but me being a preacher's kid did nothing for me getting God's blessing on my life. I had to earn God's blessings just like everyone else has to earn God's blessings. Just because your parents are spiritual does not mean that you are spiritual. The truth is, we live in a generation that simply thinks that the blessing of God on our past means that we naturally inherit those same blessings, and this is the furthest from the truth. Every person alive must earn the blessings of God on their lives. If you go down to the South in the United States you will find there are a lot of people that think they are pretty spiritual people because they live in the Bible belt. The truth of the matter is, the South is no longer the Bible belt, but truthfully needs to be belted with the Bible once again. Many of these people rely on the blessings of the past in the South, and may I say that the blessings of God are not inherited, but earned. The same can be said about our nation as a whole. America will only keep God's blessings on her when every generation in America earns the blessings of God on them. We cannot rely on the blessings of the past generations thinking that God will continue to keep His blessings upon us as a nation. The only way America will keep God's blessings upon her is to earn it by doing what **Psalm 33:12** says to do and that is, **"Blessed is the nation whose God is the LORD..."**

6. Peace with the world brings discord with God.

Here is where we start seeing the mistakes of King Solomon. Solomon never learned that you cannot be friends with the world and with God at the same time. We see in **1 Kings 3:1** that **"Solomon made affinity"** with Egypt, which is a type of the world. The word "affinity" means to make a relationship as a husband and wife make a relationship in bonding together to be married. By marrying Pharaoh's daughter, Solomon was simply trying to get along with everyone.

We must realize that you cannot be friends with God and the world at the same time. **James 4:4** says, **"Ye adulterers and adulteresses, know ye not that the friendship of the world is enmity with God? whosoever therefore will be a friend of the world is the enemy of God."** God says that it is virtually impossible for us to be a friend to God and the world. We must realize that God demands us to choose either Him or the world. Christian, if you are going to serve God, then you can count on it, you are going to offend the world and the world will hate you because it also hated Jesus. Likewise, we

111

cannot think that we can be friendly towards the world and run with the world without hurting our friendship with God. We live in a day when we try to get along with God and the world, and it never works. I am not saying that we need to be jerks towards those who live in the world and treat them rudely, but what I am saying is Christians must decide not to run in the world or associate with the activities of the world. You cannot straddle the fence and run in the world and still be a good Christian. If you are a good Christian, then you will not be a friend of the world. If you are a friend of the world, then you will not be a good Christian.

This reminds me of a dog that we had when I was a boy that always wanted to get out of the fence and run around and have his fun. I remember one day our doorbell rang and it was our neighbor informing us that our dog was stuck on top of the fence. Now this was a hard one to understand. As we walked into the back yard, we saw that our dog had climbed a four foot chain link fence and was straddling the fence when he finally realized the mess he had gotten himself into. This happens with Christians all the time. They try to straddle the fence between the world and serving God and they get stuck on the top of that fence. If we are not careful we will slip on that fence and hurt ourselves severely. Christian, you must choose which side of the fence you are going to walk on and realize you will never make the world and God happy with you at the same time. One or the other will not like what you are doing so you might as well choose sides, and may I say you ought to choose God's side and live the life He commands you to live.

7. Entertainment societies lead to falling nations.

Notice it says in **1 Kings 4:20** that Judah and Israel were many and then the Bible says they were **"…eating and drinking, and making merry."** This is nothing more than a society of people that were wrapped up in the entertainment of society. They were all about having fun and what they did not see is that this lifestyle leads to the destruction of a nation.

Study the history of the great nations and empires of the past and you will find that when these nations got wrapped up in entertainment and always having fun they ended up destroying themselves.

If all we do is wrap our lives up in how much fun we can have and in the entertainment of life, we will end up destroying ourselves and our nation. Life is not about how much fun we can have or how much entertainment we can have. Life is about people fulfilling their obligations. We live in a society that has forsaken their obligations for fun and entertainment. When you forsake your obligations you are in essence choosing to destroy yourself and your nation. Marriages that are consumed with how much fun they can have and avoid their obligation to each other will find themselves having problems in their marriage. Individuals that live for fun and will only do something if it is fun or entertaining, will find themselves never doing anything great in life. They will end up destroying themselves. The truth is, fulfilling our obligations is not always going to be fun or entertaining, but fulfilling these obligations is what will make us successful and happy in life. America needs a revival of people getting back to fulfilling their obligations. We don't need rallies about people having their rights; we need rallies about people fulfilling their obligations. Our right in life, no matter what your makeup or your background is, is to fulfill the obligations that we have entered into. For instance, a husband needs to realize being a husband and a daddy is not always going to be fun, but when you get married and have children it is your obligation to love that wife and be with her. It is your obligation to raise your children instead of running around with the guys and avoiding these obligations. You may think that this is just not fun, but you should have considered that before you ever got married and before you ever had children. Oh, the importance of our society and Christians realizing that obligation is far more important than fun and entertainment. Fulfilling our obligations in life will always lead to a life of fulfillment and happiness at the end.

8. Spiritual deterioration comes from improvements.

I am amazed at what Solomon did in the building of the temple. You will notice in **1 Kings 6:4** that Solomon had built the temple and in this temple were **"windows of narrow lights."** Nowhere in the building of the tabernacle, as you study the Bible, was there to be any windows for the temple. All the lighting of the temple was to come from the candlesticks. In even the Holy of Holies, the only lighting inside the most sacred room was to come from the Shekinah glory of God. I know to most people this seems like a very insignificant thing, but we need to understand that God did not want any outside light to light the temple or the Holy of Holies. God only wanted the lighting He prescribed. It does not matter why Solomon even put these lights in the temple. I imagine he did this with the intent to try to help the ventilation and the lighting of the temple as many have suggested, but we must also understand that God does not need man's help to do His work. It may seem like it is not that important, but if God said that the only lighting was to come from the candlesticks and from His glory, then God meant what He said. It is important because God mentioned it. If it was not important, then God would not have told them how to build the temple. You see, in Solomon's attempt to help improve the temple, he in all reality set in course the deterioration of the people of his nation. His desire to improve some things ended up changing what God had ordained.

We must understand that churches and even spiritual movements are destroyed by good and sincere people trying to improve upon what has already worked. It may not seem that important to us, but if God has told us how to do things in a certain way, then it is important to God, or else He would have never said it in the first place. We need to understand that there is nothing that God says in His Word that is unimportant. Everything in the Bible is important, otherwise it would not be there. We must be careful about trying to improve upon the things that God has told us to do. While improving these things we end up changing what we are and

114

thus become something different than what God intended for us to be. God's methods are important no matter how insignificant they may seem. You cannot improve upon God's methods. I mean, how do you improve upon the Word of God, which I believe is the King James Version 1611? Tell me, how do you improve on the local church? How do you improve on old-time preaching? How do you improve on the old-time religion? There is no way to improve on these things, and we should not try to improve on these things. Most movements are not destroyed by evil men that want to destroy the movement, but they are destroyed by good and sincere men who try to improve upon success and that which has already worked. If we are not careful, in Fundamentalism we will do the same. We will try to improve upon the paths of the old-time preachers and end up destroying Fundamentalism by improving it to its death. The methods of men from the past will still work today, and we need not change what these men have done. We need to keep on doing what they have taught us to do. Why change from what has worked and been successful in the past to something that has not been proven? I beg of every pastor, full-time Christian worker, and Christian to be careful about trying to improve on what has been handed down to us. Instead let us just keep on doing what has worked for several hundred years and not change it. In changing it, we may end up destroying the very identity of Fundamentalism.

9. The world's bluffs are just that – bluff.

You will read in **1 Kings 10:1-13** the story of the queen of Sheba coming to question Solomon. She asked him hard questions thinking that she could intimidate him with her wealth and extravagance, yet in the end it was Solomon's answers to her questions that proved that she was simply trying to bluff him. She thought she could intimidate him with her ways and her questions, but this did not happen. Solomon continued on doing what he had always done and did not change to try to impress her.

Let me say quickly that we should never let the world intimidate us into thinking that their way is better. The world's way has never been better, and just because they may flaunt their so called "education" at us, it does not mean that their way is superior to Gods' way. We should always remember that God was around before any liberal theologian was and that God's ways are not inferior to their liberal agenda. We must realize that no matter how they try to intimidate us, God's ways are proven ways. As long as we follow what God tells us to do, we need not worry about their intimidating efforts to get us to change. We must just keep doing what we have always done, realizing that at the end our ways will prove that we were and are right.

10. Extravagance always leads to discontentment.

One of the weaknesses of Solomon was that he loved to live an extravagant life and loved to flaunt his riches at people. In **1 Kings 10:14-29**, Solomon tells of all of his riches thinking that this would impress God, but the truth is those riches led to him never being happy.

We should always realize that "things" will never make a person happy, and riches will never make a person happy. The only thing that extravagant living does is it creates an appetite that will never be satisfied. I am not saying that you cannot enjoy some of the delicacies that life may afford you, but you cannot think that living an extravagant life will make you happy, for it has never made one person happy. I remember counseling a married couple that said if they just had a bigger house then they would be happy. Well, today they have a bigger house but they still are not a happy couple and are struggling in their marriage. Why? Because happiness does not come from things, happiness comes from living a right life. Happiness comes from within and not from without. If all you do is live life for the extravagant, you will always find yourself being discontent with what you have.

11. Weak associations always lead to compromise.

Notice in **1 Kings 11:4** it says **"...Solomon was old, that his wives turned away his heart after other gods..."** How did this happen to such a good man? It is simple! You will eventually become like those with whom you spend time. Whatever your weakest link is as a friend, you will eventually become this. You may be able to handle this when you are a young person, but the older you get the harder it is to fight those weak associations. You will end up becoming what you used to be against.

We must never think that we can run with weaker associations and get away with it. I could spend pages writing about people in Christianity that yoked up with people that they should not have and eventually they became like those with whom they associated. When they were younger they would preach against the very things that now they are doing. My question to these people would be, "If it was wrong when you were younger, then is it not wrong now?" Either you were wrong back then when you said it was wrong or you are wrong now! We must stop hiding behind the cloak of times changing and realize that truth never changes. People will change to be like those with whom they run.

You must never have the thought in your mind that you will run with these people so that you can change them and bring them to where you are. In the majority of the cases when someone runs with a weaker person, the weaker person tends to pull that person down instead of the stronger person pulling the weaker person up. This is why parents must be careful about thinking their child can run with a weaker child because their child will pull up that weaker person. Parents, don't ever fall for this trap! It is not your children's responsibility to try to change people, and you must realize that most likely your children will end up becoming like that weaker person. Many a parent has lost their child to the world because they let their children run with weaker associations. Their children did not change them, but the weaker associations changed that child.

117

Likewise, even preachers and adults must be careful about whom we choose to associate. You are only as strong as the weakest link of your friends. Therefore you must wisely choose friends that will pull you up and not those that have the capacity to pull you down. Don't run with people that are weaker than you. Run and associate with people that believe like you, and you will have a better chance of never compromising or changing.

12. Foolish living always brings one conclusion: God is right!

In **Ecclesiastes 12:13-14** we find the conclusion of the foolish life that Solomon lived, **"Fear God, and keep his commandments: for this is the whole duty of man. For God shall bring every work into judgment, with every secret thing, whether it be good, or whether it be evil."** After trying to see if possessions, education, wealth and fun would satisfy, Solomon came to the conclusion that keeping the commandments of God is the duty of man and that in this duty is where true happiness abides.

When it comes to the end of our lives the only thing that truly will matter is how well we obeyed God. It will not matter how many degrees we have behind our name, how much money we have in our bank accounts or even how many buildings we have built. The only thing that will truly matter is, did we accomplish what God brought us on this earth to do? Anything less than this will bring regrets in our lives.

How foolishly the life of Solomon ended. He forsook the wisdom that God had given to him and relied on his own wisdom. Look at how much talent and wisdom he wasted by doing this. I wonder what could have become of his kingdom had he taken the wisdom that God had given and followed the methods and lessons he had learned in life from his father and from God. Let us not waste the wisdom that God has given to us. Let us not become people that are filled with wisdom but live foolish lives. Instead, may we learn from the

118

lessons in Solomon's life so that we don't end up regretting a life of talent wasted on ourselves and our desires.

9

Can God Trust You?

Matthew 1:19, "Then Joseph her husband, being a just man, and not willing to make her a publick example, was minded to put her away privily."

Matthew 1:24-25, "Then Joseph being raised from sleep did as the angel of the Lord had bidden him, and took unto him his wife: And knew her not till she had brought forth her firstborn son: and he called his name JESUS."

Maybe the greatest man in the Bible aside from our Saviour Jesus Christ is Joseph, the stepfather of Jesus. Joseph is probably the most unsung hero in the entire Bible. He does not get the credit which he deserves. If I was to ask you to write down a list of the top five great men in the Bible, I could just about guarantee that Joseph's name would not end up on that list. Now this is no condemnation of you or anyone else for that matter, but it is sad that most likely the greatest man in the Bible is completely ignored. We need to understand that God trusted Joseph with His Son Jesus, and with the plan of salvation. Let me explain what I mean by telling you the story of Joseph and Mary.

Joseph and Mary were engaged to get married when the angel of God came to Mary to announce to her that she was going to bring forth a son and that this son was the Son of God who would be the Saviour of the whole world. What a shock this must have been for her to realize that she was going to be the mother of the Saviour. Yet as we read this story, Joseph finds out that his fiancée is pregnant and he knows that he is not the one that got her pregnant. In these times, if a young unmarried lady was found pregnant, she could be killed for her act of fornication. But Joseph, being a just man as the Bible calls him, instead of having her killed, decided to privately put her away. You can only imagine what was going through his mind and the emotions that Joseph was feeling at this time. We must always keep in mind that the characters of the Bible had feelings and emotions just like we do. They are human beings that God created with the same emotions and feelings that we have. I can imagine at first the shock of this news, then the anger that may have arisen in his heart, and finally, the total distrust of Mary. Can you imagine Mary trying to explain to Joseph that she was still a virgin and that this child was the Christ-child? How likely would it be for him to trust her word? Yet, while he was thinking about this, an angel of God appeared to him at night and confirmed to him what Mary had told him; she was with child of the Holy Ghost and they were to name the child Jesus. What a relief to realize that the woman whom he loved had been faithful to him and that she was still a virgin. But maybe the part that amazes me most about this story is that Joseph and Mary did get married and yet, on their honeymoon Joseph had to withhold himself from enjoying the pleasures of marriage so that Mary could be a virgin when Jesus was born. I don't know many people who would do something like this, but what trust God must have had in this couple that they would do such a thing. We must understand if they would have enjoyed the pleasures of marriage then Mary would not have been a virgin when Jesus was born, making the Bible a lie and destroying the whole plan of salvation.

What trust God must have had to actually place the entire plan of salvation in the hands of Joseph and Mary. God trusted them with our salvation, for if Joseph would have had Mary killed then Jesus would have been killed in her womb and there would be no Saviour. If Joseph would not have restrained himself from enjoying his wife the night they got married, then Mary would not have been a virgin and salvation would not be available to us. I do not know of anyone in the entire Bible who God put as much trust in as He did with Joseph and Mary. Now if God thought that Joseph could be trusted so much that He would place, literally, the plan of salvation in his hands, and even allow his Son to be raised by him, then I think we should learn about such a man and what this man was like. Let me show you over the next few pages what kind of man Joseph, this great hero of the Bible, was so that we can emulate his traits and be trusted by God to do something great for God like Joseph did.

1. He was a just man.

In **Matthew 1:19** it says, **"Then Joseph her husband, being a just man…"** As I have previously said in another chapter, the word "just" means to be a person who treats everyone fairly. It means making sure that everyone gets the same treatment and judgment and not having any favorites. Joseph, according to the Bible, was the type of man who treated everyone the same. He was a just man. He did not treat one crowd better than another because the one crowd was of a certain nationality or the one crowd had more money than the other crowd. No, Joseph was a man who was just with everyone.

It is important for us to realize that if God is going to trust us with something great in life then God, first of all, wants us to learn to be just with people. How can God ever entrust you with something great if you are not going to be fair and just with people and situations? God needs those who are going to serve Him to be just with everyone. He needs those who are going to hold positions of leadership to be fair and just with those whom they lead.

How this nation, and every nation at that, needs for its leadership to be just once again. A society that is unjust is a society that will one day destroy itself. This is why I believe that until our society gets back to being just in our judicial system, our judicial system will continue to falter in its treatment of crimes. I believe that a just judicial system should already have the punishment for a crime before the crime is committed. When someone commits a crime, they should not be sentenced by why they did this crime, by what nationality or background but they should be sentenced according to what the punishment for the crime is that was prescribed before they committed that crime. If a burglar knows if he gets caught stealing that he will get so many years no matter if this is his first time or third time, then I guarantee he will think about it before he does something. It ought not to be that if you have enough money or if you are popular enough that you can get out of the crime. It ought to be that if you break the law you pay for the law that you broke. This is what you call being just! God blesses those nations and individuals who are just people. God knows that if an individual is just with everyone and with every situation, He can trust them. If we are going to gain God's trust then we need to learn to be a just person, a person who treats everyone the same and handles every situation the same. God loves it when people are just because He is a just God Himself.

2. He was a pure young man.

As God talks about Joseph, He says in **Matthew 1:25, "And knew her not till she had brought forth her firstborn son: and he called his name JESUS."** Look at the phrase, **"knew her not..."** The Bible is telling us that Joseph had no physical relations with Mary until she had the child. This would mean that Joseph was a pure young man and a virgin young man just like Mary was.

God uses men and women who can keep themselves pure and virgin. God knows if a person can keep themselves pure He can trust them because in order to stay pure, you must keep your body and desires completely under control. It is hard to trust someone who cannot control their own physical desires with something that requires trust. Leadership requires trust, and if a person cannot control their own physical appetites and stay pure, then there is no way that they can be a good leader. One day they will hurt the hearts of those they lead because of their inability to control themselves physically. Marriage requires trust, and if you are going to marry someone, then you had better learn to trust that individual. How can you trust someone who cannot control their physical appetites before you marry them? If they cannot keep themselves pure before marriage then what will keep them faithful to you after marriage? When a young person is looking for a mate for life, they should only look for one who has kept themselves pure. I am not saying that people who were virgins when they got married will never cheat in their marriage. All I am saying is you have a better percentage of this type of person being loyal to you in marriage than one who runs around and does not worry about staying pure. God looks for people to trust, and one way God knows that He can trust an individual is by how they control their physical appetites before marriage and even after marriage. A person who cannot control themselves physically cannot be trusted with anything that requires trust.

3. He was slow to make decisions.

Notice in **Matthew 1:20** it says, **"But while he thought on these things..."** The statement alone implies that there was some time between finding out about the situation and the time that he made decisions. I believe that Joseph was a man who was not quick in making decisions. He thought on these things and took his time and, most likely, this was what his character was like in making all decisions. This is one reason why God could trust him to be the stepfather of Jesus. God knew that He could trust Joseph to make the right decisions because Joseph was not a man of quick decisions. He was a man of slow and deliberate decisions.

If you want God to be able to trust you then you need to be a person who is slow in making decisions. Learn to be very deliberate in your decision-making process. There is no way that you can trust a person with anything in life who jumps to conclusions and makes decisions quickly. I know that a person who is slow in making decisions can sometimes get annoying, but I promise you the person who is like this is a person who makes less bad decisions than the person who quickly jumps into making decisions.

When making decisions you must follow the proper principles in making decisions. When you have principles that help you in making decisions, those principles alone will slow you down. For instance, be slow in retaliation to criticism or slander. When someone has criticized you or slandered you, be very slow in responding and don't, off the spur-of-the-moment, write a scathing letter or say something quickly to get it off of your chest. You will regret this later on. Be slow when it comes to deciding about a situation. You should never make a decision about a situation by listening to only one side of the story. Before you ever make a decision about a situation you would be wise to listen to both sides of the story. Don't make your decision off of what the news media says about something for they will only give you one side of the story; the side that they want you to hear. When you hear about something on the news, reserve your judgment until you hear both sides of the story. This principle of being slow in making decisions will help you in buying a house, a car, in choosing whom to marry in life, deciding where to live and what church you should attend. God knows that those who are slow in making decisions are people whom you can trust. Be a slow and deliberate decision maker so that you can gain God's trust for something great He may have in store for you.

4. He was a man of wisdom.

Now this is really a continuation of the previous point because people who learn to be slow and deliberate in their decision making are people who are perceived as wise people and usually are wise people. Joseph was this type of man. He was wise in **Matthew 1:18-20** in how he handled the matter of Mary being pregnant. He was wise again in **Matthew 2:13-15** concerning the matter of Herod wanting to kill every man child. Joseph was a wise young man and God knew He could trust a young man who acted wisely in his decisions and in his actions.

There is no way that God can trust you with any great task if you don't learn to be wise. Of course we know that according to **James 1:5**, that God is the source of all wisdom. If you are going to get wisdom then you must have a desire and a heart to get wisdom. **Proverbs 17:16** says, **"Wherefore is there a price in the hand of a fool to get wisdom, seeing he hath no heart to it?"** God is teaching us that there is a price tag on wisdom and that price tag is called desire or having a heart for wisdom. If you are going to get wisdom then you must have desire to get that wisdom and a heart that seeks after wisdom. God promises us in **Proverbs 8:17**, if we seek after wisdom then we will get wisdom. You seek wisdom by getting to the source of wisdom and that source is the Word of God, the Bible. Unless you spend time every day in the Bible seeking the wisdom of God, you will never get that wisdom. God even says in **Proverbs 8:17**, **"I love them that love me; and those that seek me early shall find me."** God says that those who seek wisdom early in the morning will find the object that they are searching for, wisdom. God and the Bible is the source of all wisdom, and no one will ever be wise by seeking it from any other place. When a person is wise then a person can be trusted, for wise people make wise decisions and people who make wise decisions can be trusted.

5. He was a hard worker.

In **Matthew 13:55** the question was asked about Jesus, **"Is not this the carpenter's son?"** The people who asked this question were referring to Joseph. Notice they did not ask if this was the lazy man's son. They did not ask if this was the sluggard's son. They asked if this was the carpenter's son. If you have ever worked in carpentry, you will know that this is not an easy job and that those who work in this field are hard workers. Years ago, straight out of high school, I used to work in construction and I promise you, this is a hard line of work. Those who are lazy don't last long in that line of work. Joseph worked in this line of work and was a carpenter, insinuating that he was a very hard worker. God knew He

126

could trust Joseph with His Son Jesus because God saw the work ethic of Joseph and noticed that he was a hard worker.

God will never trust any man or woman who is not a hard worker. When deciding on whether to trust someone, find out what their work ethic is like and this will help you in deciding whether you can trust them. You see, a person's work ethic is a picture of their character. If a person has a good work ethic, then most likely they have good character. A person with poor work ethics who is lazy is a person you would never want to put your trust in. People who hold positions of leadership must be trusted to complete the requirements of the position that they hold. Completing your requirements requires work, and a person who is a hard worker will get it done.

If you want to find out whether or not you want to hire someone for any position, check out their work ethic and find out if they are a worker. I promise you, hard workers will work hard no matter where they are. A person who is not a hard worker in one place will not all of a sudden change and be a hard worker at another place. If you are trying to decide on whether you should marry someone or not, find out if they are a hard worker, this will help you in making your decision. If a young man is not a hard worker, then I would advise any young lady not to marry him, for he is lazy and she will end up having to work to pay the bills. No lady wants to have to carry this, as this is not her responsibility. Likewise, if a young lady is not a hard worker I would advise any young man to not marry her. If she is not a hard worker most likely she will not work to keep the house clean and you will end up living in a dump the rest of your life. I know this sounds harsh, but it is better to find these things out before and not after. A person's work ethic will always tell you whether they can be trusted or not.

6. He was a thinker.

Notice again in **Matthew 1:20** it says, **"But while he thought on these things..."** Joseph was a man who thought about

127

things. He was not a man who had to have others think for him. He was a man who thought for himself. Again, here is another reason why God could trust him to raise Jesus because God wanted a person to raise Jesus who did not always have to be entertained; God wanted a person to raise Jesus who knew how to think.

Leaders are thinkers! You will never assume any quality leadership role in life without being a thinker. Our society is filled with people who want others to think for them. You will find that the entertainment business as a whole is one of the most profitable businesses in society today. What a shame! This would mean that as a whole, our society is filled with people who let others think for them and they don't think for themselves. What an indictment against our society. If you ever aspire to be a leader, and a quality leader at that, then you must learn to be a thinker. Look at those who are leaders and you will realize that they have to be thinkers to do their jobs. Preachers have to be thinkers. Coaches have to be thinkers. Teachers have to be thinkers. If you plan on being a good parent then you must be a thinker. You cannot allow yourself to fall trap to the mode of letting everyone else think for you, you must learn to be a thinker and learn to think for yourself. Spend time reading books. While you read you are thinking. Spend time meditating on the Bible and on life in general and you will find that in order to meditate you must think. One of the qualities that you should look for in a person who you want to trust is the same quality that God looks for in a person that He chooses to trust and that is, they must be a thinker.

7. He was a man of obedience.

Matthew 1:24 says, **"Then Joseph being raised from sleep did as the angel of the Lord had bidden him, and took unto him his wife:"** Joseph was a man who knew how to obey God and obey the rules that God had given to him. God told him to marry Mary, and according to this verse, he did just that. God told Joseph to name the child Jesus, and Joseph named the child what God told him to name the child. Joseph could be trusted because he was a man who was obedient to the rules that God gave to him.

A person who cannot follow the rules cannot be trusted. If you would like for God to trust you with something great in life then you had better learn how to be obedient and follow the rules. I like to play golf, or maybe I should say, I like to participate in golf. I don't know that you would call what I do playing golf. When I do get a chance to play some golf, I always inform those that I play with that I will only play with them if they don't take mulligans when they are playing. In the rules of golf there is no such thing as getting one free shot if you have a bad shot. This is called cheating! I have said for years that I can find out a lot about a person by taking them golfing. I watch people who I have played with move the ball to get a better lie and then not count it as a stroke. This is nothing more than cheating! I've learned that I cannot trust those who take mulligans. If they will skirt the rules when playing golf, then they will skirt the rules in life and those rules are there for a reason. God uses those who follow the rules and are obedient to the rules of life because God knows He can trust individuals like this.

8. He had faith in God's Word.

Think with me just a bit as Joseph is informed that his wife is pregnant and that the child in her womb was placed there by God. What trust in God's Word this took as this had never been heard of before and truthfully it sounded a little far fetched. Yet, Joseph had faith because God said that this was true. Certainly when God saw that Joseph was willing to trust His Word no matter how ridiculous and far fetched it may seem, God knew that He could trust a person such as this to raise His Son Jesus.

God will never trust you with something big if you can't have faith that God is right when He tells you to do something from His Word. Let me be quite honest with you, it takes faith to

129

believe God's Word. It takes faith to follow God's commands. There will be times, when God uses you, He will ask you to do something that truthfully will seem like it is ridiculous or a little far fetched, but you must have faith that God's Word is true and not trust your own opinions. If God cannot trust you to do something that seems ridiculous then God cannot trust you at all. It takes faith in God's Word for God to learn to trust you.

9. He was faithful to his wife.

Luke 2:41 says, **"Now his parents went to Jerusalem every year at the feast of the passover."** Notice it says that Jesus' parents went together to the feast of the Passover. I believe that this implies that Joseph was not only a good family man but also a man who was faithful to his wife. Nowhere in the Bible does it ever give us any reason to doubt that Joseph was unfaithful to his wife. They had several children and seemed to be a close family. God knew that if Joseph would be faithful to his wife then Joseph was a man who could be trusted.

Let me just say that if you can't be faithful to the one that you married then there is no way that God can trust you to do something great for Him. Marriage in itself requires trust, and if you break the trust in marriage then how in the world do you expect God to trust you? Let me just add this, you may still be married and you may be cheating on your mate, but God does see this and He knows how much He can trust you by how faithful you are to your mate. It is not a matter of whether you have been caught or not. God can see you no matter where you are. Your vows of marriage are vows of trust, and when those vows are broken, you have also broken any trust that God could have in you.

10. He was faithful to church.

Referring back to **Luke 2:41**, you will notice that they went yearly to the feast of the Passover. This would mean that they were faithful to church. Joseph could be trusted because he was faithful to church.

How do you expect God to trust you if you can't be faithful to your church services each week? Not only should you be faithful to church each week, but faithful to every church service as well. Your faithfulness to church is a great way to show God that you are worthy to be trusted. Listen, you need to stop looking for excuses and reasons to miss church. Stop using lame excuses for your unfaithfulness to church. I am talking about excuses like, sickness, your child is sick, the job, being tired, holidays, family visiting from out of town, and many other excuses. I could never have enough time and space to give all the reasons why people say they miss church. You should not look for reasons to miss church; you should be looking for reasons to attend church. God will never use you if you are not faithful to church. If you can't be trusted to be faithful to church, then there is no way you can be trusted with any other task that God would like to give to you.

11. He believed in second chances.

I love this about Joseph and I believe that God loved this about Joseph. In **Matthew 1:19** Joseph was not wanting to make a public example out of Mary, instead he just wanted to put her away privately so that she could put her life back together. Now this is the type of person whom you can trust.

God looks for people who believe that others can have a second chance when they mess up their lives. God knows that He can trust individuals who are not quick to gossip and tear down those that have fallen into sin. Instead, the individuals that take those who have messed up their lives in sin and try to put their lives together are people who can be trusted. How important it is that we become a trusted individual whom people know they can come to when they mess up their lives, because they know we won't gossip about them and tear them down, but they trust that we will help them

131

put their lives back together because we believe in second chances. You see, God knows when a person believes in second chances that this person has become more like Him because God is a God who gives second chances. God knows that a person who has become more like Him in this area is a person who He can trust, for they have taken on His characteristics. Anyone who has the characteristics of God can be trusted, for God can be trusted. Don't be a person who, when you hear of someone falling, rejoices or you are quick to tell others. Be a person who believes no matter what a person does, God can still remake that person into someone whom He can use again. In so doing, you will become a person who God can trust.

12. He treated his stepchild as though he was his own child.

As you read in **Luke 2:48**, you will notice as Mary responds to Jesus she says, **"...Son, why hast thou thus dealt with us? behold, thy father and I have sought thee sorrowing."** Notice that it bothered Joseph as well as Mary that Jesus seemed to be lost. It says that they both were sorrowful about losing the child. A person like Joseph who is just as concerned with their stepchild as they are their own child is certainly someone who can be trusted. This is a sign of their character. You see, character does what its responsibilities are and when you get married to an individual who already has a child, then your responsibility is to take care of that child the same way you would take care of your own children. This is character, and again, God can trust people with character and so can you.

I am very sure as I write this book that there will be people who will read this book who have remarried or have married into a situation where either the husband or the wife will have to help raise a child that is not their own child. Now may I say to those who have this great responsibility, you ought to treat that child as your own child. One of the great characteristics of Joseph was that he took care of Jesus as if he was his own child. I have run across both sides of this story. I hear about people who just want to send their stepchild off to some boarding school because they want nothing to do with the child, and this is a shame. When you married that person you also married their children. You should not treat your own children any better than you treat your mates' children who are not yours. Then there are times when I do run across individuals who tell me their mate treats their stepchildren as their own children. My, the confidence and trust this gives to their mate and that child. If you are living in a situation like this and you would like for God to use you in a great way, then why don't you prove yourself trustworthy to God? Fulfill your responsibility to take care of your stepchildren as well you would your own child.

13. He was a godly man.

Let me remind you concerning this point, that three times we see Joseph hearing the voice of God's messengers talking to him. We see this in **Matthew 1:20**, **Matthew 2:13** and again in **Matthew 2:19-20**. Joseph was a godly man, for in order to hear God's message to him he had to be close enough to God to hear the messenger speak.

Godly people are people who can be trusted. Let me ask you this question, are you known to God as a godly person or are you known to God as a worldly person? Notice I did not say do you think you are a godly person. I asked you what God knows you as. This is important! It matters not what you think of yourself or what others think of you, it only matters what God *KNOWS* about you. Listen; can your ears hear the world's cry better than they can hear the voice of God? Are you more open to the desires and cries of the world than you are to God's voice speaking to you? Does the cry of the world's desires drown out the voice of God in your ears? People whom God will trust are people who are godly people whose ears are open to the voice of God because they walk with Him daily in His Word.

14. He was a man whom God could trust.

This goes without saying as I have emphasized this over and over again in this chapter: Joseph was a man whom God could trust. God could trust Joseph because he was a man who practiced self-restraint. God could trust Joseph because he proved himself trustworthy.

Have you proved yourself trustworthy to God? Does your life exemplify the same qualities as Joseph's life which caused God to trust him? If today God was looking for someone to raise Jesus, could He trust you to do it because you have proven yourself trustworthy? What trust God had in Joseph and Mary to literally entrust the Gospel to them. No wonder God chose Joseph to be the stepfather of Jesus. Truly Joseph, who is an unsung hero in the Bible, proved to God that God could trust Him, and trust him God did. Why not strive to be trusted of God so He will trust you with something this big!

10

Finding Grace with God

Genesis 6:8, "But Noah found grace in the eyes of the LORD."

When I think of the favorite Bible stories that I heard as a child, one of the stories that I remember the most is the story of Noah and the ark. Other than the story of David and Goliath, probably the most popular story worldwide is the story of Noah and the ark.

Noah lived in a very wicked generation. The people of the world in his day lived for themselves, entertainment and nothing else. The Bible says in **Genesis 6:5, "And GOD saw that the wickedness of man was great in the earth, and that every imagination of the thoughts of his heart was only evil continually."** As God looked over the world everything that He saw in the world was wicked. It was not just in the people's actions, but even every thought of their hearts was wicked and evil. The Bible tells us that God decided that He was going to destroy the earth in 120 years. Now why did God give the earth that many years before He was going to destroy it? I believe that God was hoping that maybe man in those 120 years would turn around and come back to Him. God was simply giving man a space of 120 years to come back to Him so that He could stop His judgment. Yet there was one man upon the earth who did find grace in God's eyes, and this man was Noah. Noah was the only man in all the earth that God could find doing right. Because of this, Noah found grace in God's eyes. What a testimony to the greatness of this man. God then came to Noah to reveal to him what He was going to do to the world. Then God commanded Noah to build an ark so that He could preserve him from the flood. Noah embarked upon the great undertaking of building this massive ark because God was going to send His judgment in the form of a great flood upon the earth. Oh, we must understand how much Noah trusted God, for there had never been rain upon the earth before. Even though Noah did not know what rain was, he knew if God said this was going to happen then it was going to happen. Imagine, for 120 years Noah built this ark without one time seeing any raindrops fall from the sky. Yet he never gave up on his faith that God was going to do what He said He was going to do. Then finally the day came when His faith in God was proven to be true; God sent the flood upon the whole earth. Now let me just add this to this portion of the story, there are some who would say that the flood only covered the part of the earth that Noah lived in, and this is completely false. The Bible says that the waters covered the face of the earth, meaning that the whole earth was covered up in water just like God said would happen. Noah and his family were saved from this flood because of his faith in God and because Noah found grace in the eyes of God. If Noah was the type of individual who God singled out, then I think that we should learn about this man. Let us find out what we can do to help our own lives. Let me give you some lessons that we can learn from the life of Noah.

1. Living a right life is a choice.

Though Noah lived in a very wicked generation, Noah still found himself doing what was right in the eyes of God. You must understand that even the family of Noah did not live a life that could find grace in God's eyes. I believe that his grandfather, Methuselah, died in the flood. When you do the math of how many years he lived on the earth and then look at when the flood happened, you will find that Methuselah died the very same year as the flood. Now I do not believe it is a coincidence that God put this in the Bible. Even if Methuselah did not die in the flood, we do know one thing for certain, Methuselah did not find grace in the eyes of God. This can only mean one thing, that God included him in the category of those who did wickedness and evil. Think about

136

this: Noah was the only one in the entire world that was doing right!

Yes, it was a choice for Noah to do right just like it is also a choice for people to do wrong. If there was ever a person who had the excuse of peer pressure causing them to do wrong, Noah had that excuse. Instead, Noah would not use that excuse to do wrong and made a conscience choice to do right. This is why he made it through the flood. You see, it matters not what your background is or what others around you are doing, you are ultimately responsible for your own actions. Noah realized that it was his choice as to what type of life he was going to live and he refused to let others influence him into what type of life to live. Noah did right, not because it was popular, but Noah did right because it was right to do. This is exactly what you must decide to do if you are going to find grace in God's eyes. You must not look at what everyone else is doing and you must look at what is right to do and do that which is right. If your family is not serving God, you must still serve God. If your church decides to do wrong, you must still decide to do right. If the friends around you stop doing what is right, you must still do what is right for right is always the right thing to do. If you do right only because it is popular, then you will find yourself one day doing wrong because someday right will not be the popular thing to do. I can remember one day I was sitting in the office of my good friend Dr. Jeff Owens, who is now my pastor, and he made a statement to me that was a huge compliment. He said, "Bro. Domelle, I know I don't have to worry about you changing your preaching because you don't preach the way you do because it is popular, but you preach the way you do because you believe it is right." Oh, what a compliment this was! Yet this is the only reason why a person will live a right life. If you are going to live right on the job, in the school, or any place then you must do right when it is popular and when it is not popular. Living right is a choice that you must make. Sometimes this choice will not be popular and will cause you to lose friends of a lifetime and family, but you still must do right.

2. Only God's grace can please God.

You will see that there was only one thing that caused Noah to avoid the judgment of God; he found God's grace. Our text verse, **Genesis 6:8** says, **"But Noah found grace in the eyes of the LORD."** Now you will notice that Noah had to make the decision to get God's grace and God did not give His grace until Noah asked for it. You see, God's grace was there, but it was up to Noah to find that grace and then take that grace. That same grace was there for everyone else but Noah was the only one who took that grace. It was this grace that Noah found and took that allowed him to avoid the judgment of God.

What a wonderful story of salvation we find here in the story of Noah and the ark. You see, it is only through grace that a person can even be saved. **Ephesians 2:8-9** says, **"For by grace are ye saved through faith; and that not of yourselves: it is the gift of God: Not of works, lest any man should boast."** It was not the works of Noah that kept him from God's judgment. It was not the sacraments of some church that kept Noah from the judgment of God. It was nothing but the grace of God that kept Noah from facing the judgment of God. The same is true with us. The only way that we as humans can avoid the judgment of God is through His grace. Our works cannot save us and take us to Heaven and neither can our church or our church's sacraments or anything other than accepting the grace of God that He offers through His Son Jesus Christ. If a person is going to avoid the judgment of God and make it to Heaven, then they are going to do it because of God's grace that He gives to us through His Son Jesus. It is only through His grace that we can please God. This is why a person needs to have a specific time when they have put their faith in Christ's payment for their sins upon the cross. This is the ONLY WAY that a person can find grace in God's eyes and anything less than God's grace will not please God.

3. A balanced life comes from walking with God.

Notice in **Genesis 6:9** that is says that **"...Noah was a just man and perfect in his generations..."** The word "perfect" in this verse in not implying that Noah was sinless, but rather this word means that Noah was a complete or well-balanced individual. It is saying that Noah, in his generation, was a balanced individual or a person who was well-rounded in everything that he did in life. How did he achieve this? The verse continues on and shows us how he achieved this; he **"...walked with God."** Walking with God made him a balanced individual.

May I say that the same is true with you and me; the only way we will ever become well-balanced people is by walking with God. The goal that God has for all of us is to be well-balanced in everything that we do. This is one reason why we must spend time walking with God in the Bible. The Bible is one of the tools that helps us become a well-balanced individual. You will see in **2 Timothy 3:16-17, "All scripture is given by inspiration of God, and is profitable for doctrine, for reproof, for correction, for instruction in righteousness: That the man of God may be perfect, throughly furnished unto all good works."** One of the purposes of the Bible is to produce well-balanced people and not people who are lopsided individuals. This is why without the Bible an education cannot be well-balanced. The Bible is the source of all wisdom and without the Bible a person will never achieve a balanced life. A balanced life is the only life that will bring contentment, happiness and joy. Oh, how important it is for us to walk with God. It is only through our walk with God that God furnishes us and makes us balanced. This verse tells us that the Bible was given to us to **"throughly furnish"** us so that we may do His good works. You see the Bible is like furniture. People fill their house with furniture and supplies so that they can live a comfortable life inside of their house. Can you imagine having a house with only a couple of rooms furnished with furniture and the rest of the rooms are empty with only walls to look at and nothing else useful about them? Well, this is what God wants us to avoid in our lives in not being perfect or well-balanced people. God's desire is that every facet of our life is balanced so that we are useful in all areas of life. God does not want parts of our lives to be wasted spaces. The only way you will ever accomplish having a balanced life and being furnished in all areas of your life is through walking with God and by reading His Word.

4. A father's first responsibility is to his family.

Look at God's command to Noah in **Genesis 7:1** when God tells Noah that he and his family were to go into the ark. God did not want Noah to have no concern for the world. God did not want Noah to leave his family to die and go to Hell. God was teaching us the importance of reaching our own family first. Notice the progression of making sure that we do right. God first of all told Noah to get into the ark, and then to bring his family into the ark, and then you see God addresses him about the generation that he lived in, which was others. The first person we need to be concerned about going to Heaven is ourself. We need to first of all make sure that we are saved! Then after we get saved, we need to make sure that our family members get saved so that they can go to Heaven with us. Then last of all, we are to take this Gospel to our generation, or the rest of the world, and make sure they have the truth of the Gospel to make the choice of whether they will go to Heaven or not.

What a shame it would be if a person is so concerned about the rest of the world that they forget to get their own family saved. You show me how much you witness to your lost family members and I will show you how much you truly care for the lost. Sometimes the hardest people to witness to are those in our own family and yet God says that after we take care of ourselves we should then make sure our families are taken care of and are saved. Don't be guilty of trying to reach the world for Christ and let your own family members die and go to Hell because you just would not witness to them.

Let me also take this one step further and say we are first responsible for doing right ourselves and living a right life. Then the next step is to be concerned with our families doing right and living a right life. After you do this, that is, get your family saved and living right, then go to the world and try to get them to live right. What a shame it would be for you to lose your family for the sake of trying to reach the world. I don't believe it has to be this way. I really believe that we can reach our family and the world also. We must be careful that we don't get so wrapped up in trying to do our ministries in reaching the world for Christ that we lose our own families. Now let me say, I am not trying to give you a crutch to be lazy and not get involved in the ministries of the church. I believe everyone should be involved in some ministry in their church. All that I am trying to get you to understand is that while you are trying to reach the world, don't forget to reach your own family also. Noah's first responsibility was to go after his family.

5. A fear of God is a great motivator to do right.

It is interesting that in **Hebrews 11:7** it says, **"...By faith Noah, being warned of God of things not seen as yet, moved with fear, prepared an ark to the saving of his house..."** Notice it was the fear of what God could do that motivated Noah to build the ark. Sometimes fear is a good thing because fear will motivate us to do right. It was Noah's fear of God's judgment that caused Noah to build the ark. He did not build the ark just because he had nothing else to do. He built that ark because God said He was going to destroy the earth and the only way Noah would be delivered from this judgment would be to build the ark and get on that ark. It was a fear of God that motivated Noah to do right.

Let me say that a true fear of God will always cause a person to do what is right. Now when I say a fear of God, let me explain by using a very vivid illustration. Most people fear electricity and rightfully so. Years ago I traveled in a fifth wheel trailer with my wife, going to our revival meetings. In

141

just about every church I had to wire into the circuit breaker box so that I could hook up electricity to my fifth wheel trailer. Many times a pastor would ask me if I wanted him to cut off all the electricity and my response was always, no. I told him I would be fine as long as he did not get close to me and no one else got close to me. When I would go into the circuit breaker box and wire into the box for my trailer I was always so very careful. I knew that the electricity in that box could injure me, and even kill me, if I did not fear what was in that box. The power in that box demanded of me to fear what it could do to me if I did not use it right. But, the same power that could injure or kill me could also help me as long as I kept it in the right perspective. I had to respect what it could do to me if I became careless. The same is true with God! We must and should have a fear of God! We should fear what His power can do to us if we don't do what is right. If we treat God right and respect the power that He has, then the same power that can hurt us can help us to do great things for Him. You see, that is what a true fear of God is: it is respecting what the power can do if we use it incorrectly and what the power can help us accomplish when we use it wisely. Christians need to get back to having a fear of God. The proper perception of God's fear will motivate us to do right. When we do right, then that same power that we fear can help us to accomplish great things for God. Oh, Christian, don't ever become so comfortable about God's power that you just take it for granted and end up hurting yourself. Always fear what God can do if you don't do right and use that fear to motivate you to do what is right.

6. The response of people should not change the message of God.

Notice again in **Hebrews 11:7** that Noah's message did not change though the world had not responded. Do you understand how long Noah must have preached this message? Not only did he preach the message that God was going to destroy the world in 120 years, but Noah was just under 500 years old when God told him that He was going to destroy the world. This would mean that for hundreds of years Noah preached righteousness though man did not respond. He did not change his message because it was not popular or because he was not getting the response he wanted, instead he just kept on preaching the truth of God to the world whether they wanted to hear it or not.

As preachers or teachers of God we should never change the message that God has given to us because it is not popular or because we are not getting the response that we want. Popularity is not the purpose of preaching truth. We preach the truth because God tells us to preach the truth. We must be careful, in this day of political correctness, that we don't let what the world wants to hear change the message of God. I am fed up with the liberal preachers who will not preach the truth because it is just not popular. What this generation needs are men of God like Noah who preach the truth no matter how popular it is and continue preaching it even if it means that people stop coming to our churches. If we must preach the truth and only have a small crowd of people come, then let's preach the truth. If we change our message to get a crowd then God pity us! We should never preach something just because it is popular and what everyone wants to hear. We should preach what God tells us to preach even if it means that no one will follow us and we alone are the only one preaching the truth.

7. Time vindicates righteousness.

Imagine Noah preaching for 120 years that God was going to judge the world with a flood and for the entire 120 years not one raindrop fell from the sky. You can just imagine the criticism and the negative thoughts about Noah. I am very confident that most people just thought Noah was some crazy old preacher who didn't know what he was talking about. But in **Genesis 7:16-17** the Bible says, **"And they that went in, went in male and female of all flesh, as God had commanded him: and the LORD shut him in. And the flood was forty days upon the earth; and the waters**

143

increased, and bare up the ark, and it was lift up above the earth." Finally, after 120 years of preaching that the judgment of God was going to come, it finally came. Time finally vindicated Noah and his righteous living. Six hundred years of righteous living finally paid off. For six hundred years he lived right in a wicked environment and now finally it all paid off when God saved him and killed everyone else.

We need to keep in mind that time will always vindicate our righteous living. People around us may criticize us, but when living right, we need to remember that time is on our side and eventually time will prove that we are right and they are wrong. I can remember my parents, for so many years, had rules that our family had to live by. Many times people would tell my parents that they were going to run us kids off. Well, after all of these years I would say my parents have been vindicated for how they raised us, for now they have two children in the ministry and the other two are hard-working decent citizens in society. Many of those who criticized them have seen their own children get into trouble with the law, have trouble with drugs and alcohol and many of them ended up with destroyed marriages. It was not always easy for my parents to keep the rules in the house, but they did. Time has finally vindicated them and shown those who criticized them that they were right in raising their kids the way that the Bible tells parents to raise their children. Don't ever think that your righteous living is in vain, for God promises in **Galatians 6:7, "Be not deceived; God is not mocked: for whatsoever a man soweth, that shall he also reap."** You must take courage that God will eventually vindicate you for doing what is right. Don't give up hope for living right. It may seem that doing right does not pay, but time will eventually prove you right, so just hang in there and don't give up.

8. The greatest test of your Christianity is whether or not your family will follow you.

The greatest test, and the one that showed the greatness of this man Noah, was when his family in **Genesis 7:7** followed him into the ark with their wives. Noah was already a great man whether or not his family followed him, but his greatness was magnified by the fact that his family saw that he was right and was willing to take the same criticisms of the world and follow him into the ark. Though they knew his weaknesses, as every family will know each others weaknesses, he was real enough to them that they were willing to follow him into the ark. This most certainly was a great test of his Christianity.

The greatest test of your Christianity is whether or not your family is willing to follow you as you serve God. You show me how good of a Christian your family thinks your are and I will show you how good of a Christian your truly are. It matters not how good of a Christian you say you are, but when those who live with you say you are a good Christian, then that is a testament to your Christian life. You see, you may be able to cover up all of your weaknesses to everyone else, but your family knows who you truly are. When they say that you are a great Christian then this is most certainly one of the greatest tests of how good a Christian you truly are. Not only this, but when your family is willing to follow you, this only magnifies your testimony. We all need to ask ourselves what kind of Christian does our family think we are and if our answer is negative then we need to change some things in our lives. The best funerals that I like to perform are the ones when I talk to the family members and they say that their loved one was truly a great Christian. Don't worry about being a legend in your own mind and try to convince yourself and others how good a Christian you are, live a right life in front of your family and do what is right in front of them and they will tell others what a good Christian you truly are.

9. The safest place to be is in God's will.

Genesis 7:23 says, "…and Noah only remained alive, and they that were with him in the ark." Noah was safe as long as he stayed inside of the ark which was the will of God for his life. If Noah would have left the ark, though he was a saved man, Noah would have lost his life. The safest place for Noah to be was right in the center of the will of God, which for him was in the ark.

The same is true for each one of us! The safest place a Christian can live is in the place that is God's will for their life. If God's will is in a dangerous land where they could be killed, then that land is safer for them than in their own country living close to their parents and friends. It matters not how bad a place is, if it is God's will for your life, then that place will be the safest place for you to live. Parents, don't you fall trap to the Devil's lie when your children are trying to follow the will of God and go to some foreign mission land that is not the safest place. When you try to stop them you are fighting against God and fighting for the Devil. I do not think you want to be a part of that. My parents have always taught me that the safest place that I can ever live is wherever God wants me to live. This is true even if humanly speaking, it is a dangerous place. Safety is not where I want to live but safety is in the will of God for my life. This is why when a soul winner goes soul winning in a dangerous neighborhood they are safer doing this than playing ball in a safe neighborhood when they should have been soul winning. God's will is the safest place. If we do get injured or killed in the will of God, that was a safer place than being out of the will of God. I would rather die in God's will doing right than to stay alive outside of God's will, for then I must face the judgment of God. We must always remember that safety is not determined by what man calls safe, but safety is inside God's will for our lives. Safety is doing what He has commanded for us to do, for inside of this will we will be delivered from the floods of God's judgment.

10. God enjoys a thankful heart.

You will notice in **Genesis 8:20-21** that after Noah left the ark he set up an altar to sacrifice to God for delivering him and his family from the flood. The sacrifice was a sacrifice of thanks to God. We notice that this sacrifice of thanks was a sweet-smelling savour to God.

God always enjoys a thankful heart. Every Christian should learn to be thankful to God for all that He has done for them. But you will notice that it was after Noah thanked God that God promised to never again destroy the earth with a flood. Why was it after he had given thanks to God? Because being thankful to God will always cause God to do more for those who are thankful. We should never take for granted the blessings of God. We should learn to always be thankful to God for what He has done for us so that we can keep those blessings coming our way. Don't you think that God will bless those who thank Him more than those who never thank Him? I want to live such a life that as soon as God gives me some blessing, I run to Him to thank Him for His goodness to me so that He will want to continue to give me those blessings. Maybe the reason why some people get more blessings from God than others is because some people thank God for those blessings more than others. Now I think we all should thank God for His blessings by audibly thanking Him, but I also think that one of the greatest ways we can show our gratitude to God for what He has done for us is to live for Him and do more for Him. I think that when God sees that every time He blesses me I do something for Him, He is more inclined to keep those blessings coming my way than if I never did anything at all. Don't ever find yourself being an ungrateful Christian who never thanks God for His goodness you. Truthfully, God has been very good to all of us and we could never even touch His goodness to us if we tried.

11. God's grace is not a license to sin.

I hate to end this chapter this way but I cannot leave out a part of the life of Noah from which we can learn some valuable lessons. We see in **Genesis 9:20-23** that Noah had a vineyard that he had grown and one night he took the wine of this vineyard and got drunk. While he was drunk we learn that Noah committed a sin with his own son and God ended up cursing this son for doing such a thing with his dad. What a shame that Noah ended up putting a blot on the story of his life by thinking that God's grace, that he had found, gave him a license to do wrong.

Listen, you never earn the right to sin no matter what you have done. The past success of Noah did not give him a right to do wrong and the past success that you have had in your life does not give you a right to do wrong. God's grace on our lives does not give us a license to sin, but God's grace on our lives should cause us to live right. Just because we are saved by grace and now can no longer lose that salvation, this does not give us a license to go out and do whatever we want to do. No, sin still has a price and our committing of that sin will cause us to have to pay the price for what we have done. We should never think that we can get away with doing wrong because God has been so gracious to us. Just like God punished Noah and his son for their sin, God likewise will punish us for any sin that we have done. God's grace, which He has so mercifully given to us, is not a license for us to go and do anything we want! We always need to keep in mind that God has been gracious to us. Because of this grace we should want to show Him our gratitude by not prostituting this grace by doing wrong. Instead, do what He asks you to do, for what better way can we show our appreciation to God for His grace than to do what He asks us to do? God's grace does not give us a license to not go to church, but God's grace should compel us to want to go to church. God's grace does not give us a license to have immoral thoughts, but God's grace should motivate us to live moral lives and have moral thoughts. God's grace is not a license to sin. His grace should be the tool that causes us to want to do right and serve Him with the rest of our lives.

Noah found grace with God. This grace caused Noah to do many things that should teach us how to live our lives daily. We should take these lessons from the life of Noah and imitate them in our lives so that we can get God's grace to fall upon us, not for salvation, but for daily living.

11

A Man of God

2 Kings 1:9-10, "Then the king sent unto him a captain of fifty with his fifty. And he went up to him: and, behold, he sat on the top of an hill. And he spake unto him, Thou man of God, the king hath said, Come down. And Elijah answered and said to the captain of fifty, If I be a man of God, then let fire come down from heaven, and consume thee and thy fifty. And there came down fire from heaven, and consumed him and his fifty."

The need of every generation is found in the life of the prophet Elijah; every generation needs a man of God. I am not talking about someone who calls himself a man of God because they pastor a church or carry the title of the leader of their denomination. What I am talking about is a true man of God, a man that is in touch with God and has the power of God upon his life like the prophet Elijah had.

As we study the life of Elijah, we know that he was a man of God. We don't know anything about the childhood of Elijah. We do not know who his parents were. We don't know if his parents were rich or poor, if they were spiritual parents that reared him right, or even if they were parents that were ungodly. The only thing we know is that Elijah was called the Tishbite, which would mean that he came from the city of Tishbi in the region of Gilead. It is interesting to me, that though we know nothing about where he came from or his background, God knew exactly where he was. In God's timing God introduced him to the nation of Israel during a very needy time for that nation. The king of Israel, King Ahab, was a wicked king. God introduced him as a national spiritual leader when He told Elijah to go to King Ahab and prophesy that there would be a famine in the land for three years, and his prophecy came to pass.

What is interesting to me is how every generation of people wonders who will be the next national spiritual leader. Many times people will speculate who the next leader will be. Other times you will see people jockey for that position, yet in every case God raises up a leader for each generation. More likely than not, the leader God chose was not on anybody's list to be the national leader. You see, God does not look at whom people think should be the next leader; God knows whom He has groomed for that position and whom He can trust to carry out that position.

For Israel, that person was Elijah. Elijah was not someone whom everybody would have put on their list to be the next leader. He seemed to be the most unlikely person to become that leader. Why? First, because he lacked notoriety in the nation of Israel. Nobody even knew who he was. Second, he was an unlikely leader because of how strange his appearance was. He did not dress in the fine clothing that the average national leader would dress in; instead he wore a leather girdle made of sheepskin. Later on we find out that this leather girdle became the main storyline in the life of Elisha. Elisha picked up the mantle of Elijah, which was that leather girdle. Elijah's personal appearance would seem to be a little rough and would not fall into the mold of what you would expect from a prophet. Though Elijah had all of this against him, God was the one that lifted him up and set him on the stage. The good thing about God setting him up is when God sets a person up no man can destroy him or his ministry because man did not make him, God did! God was the only One Who could choose to take him down. You will notice that Elijah did not have to promote himself to become the next leader. God lifted him up because God knows where everyone lives, and he knows everyone's name. If it is in God's plan to make someone a national leader, then God knows where to find them. We don't need people to promote themselves to prominence; we need people that will simply do what God has called of them to do. If God wants to promote them then He will know where to find them. Oh, the need for every generation to have a man of God.

I can remember sitting in the office of my preacher, Dr. Jack Hyles, and telling him my desire to do more for God, not to become a well known preacher, but to help the cause of Christ. I remember the wise counsel he gave to me that most certainly saved my ministry from being destroyed. He said, "Bro. Domelle, don't try to get big, for when you try to get big you will end up changing for the sake of getting big." He said to me, "God knows your name and God knows your telephone number and He even knows where you live." He said, "What you need to do is just stay busy doing what you are supposed to do and in God's timing He will make you bigger if He chooses to make you bigger." He then for the next ten to fifteen minutes told me about men that wanted to get bigger and now they have changed from what they used to be all because of their desire to get big and become that national leader. I do not know if God will ever use you in a national way, but I do know there are several lessons that we can learn about Elijah the man of God. We can all apply these lessons to our lives, and that will make us better people and, most of all, better Christians.

1. He was not afraid to stand alone.

As you look at the life of Elijah, the one story that stands out more than any other story is when he challenged the false prophets of Baal to a contest to see whose God could send fire down from Heaven. In this story you will find many of the characteristics of this great man of God. One of the characteristics that helped him to be such a great man of God was that he was not afraid to stand alone. In **1 Kings 18:22** Elijah makes a statement to the people by saying, **"...I, even I only, remain a prophet of the LORD; but Baal's prophets are four hundred and fifty men."** Is it not interesting that he was the only one among over four hundred people that was willing to stand up for God? He was not standing because it was the most popular thing to do; he was standing because it was the right thing to do. This could be one of the main reasons why God chose him to be a spiritual leader for his generation. God knew that He would need to find someone who was not intimidated by the size of the crowd and who would not let the crowd dictate what he would preach, how he would act or what he would do. Elijah was a true man who knew that standing for truth was more important than fame or popularity. He was not worried about being accepted by man. He was concerned with being accepted by God.

No person will ever be used by God who cannot learn to stand alone. The true test of a person and their character is how they stand when they are the minority and especially when they are the only one that is standing for what is right. You might as well cross yourself off of the list to be used by God in a great way if you must depend on the crowd to decide what you are going to do. I can recall when I was just a young man, I worked at a paper factory, and for awhile I was the only Christian in the whole work place. On one Saturday during the summertime, I was supposed to work some overtime along with several other men in order to get an order finished that had come in. On our lunch break when I went to the lunch room to have lunch, I saw many of the men bringing their coolers in and they were loaded with beer. They all went to the outside of the lunchroom where there was a horseshoe pit and they began to drink their beer and I stayed inside. One young man about nineteen years of age came in with a beer in his hand and offered me a beer. I told him that I was not interested in drinking any beer and that he might as well go out with the rest of the men because I would not partake in this event. He proceeded to tell me that my parents would never find out and that I should go ahead and try a drink. I again told him I would not do such a wicked thing for it did not matter if my parents found out, I told him that my God would know if I drank and that was more important to me than my parents not knowing about it. He again tried to get me to drink and then tried to force a drink down my lips. I quickly grabbed a wooden triangle that was on the pool table in the lunchroom and hit him over the head with it. He looked at me and asked me why I did this and I told him that I intended to never have a drop of alcohol touch my lips, and if he was going to try to force me, I would fight him over it. I do not know if this was what caught God's attention regarding me or not, but I do believe that God saw that I was willing to stand alone, and because of this God decided to use me to the extent that I have been used up to this day.

It is mighty important that if you ever plan on being used by God that you learn to stand alone for right and not worry about what the crowd says. Be concerned with what God wants. We need men who will learn to stand alone and lead their families down the paths of righteousness. We need Christians who will learn to stand for right on the job and close their ears to the criticisms of their work partners and open their ears to the compliments of a job well done by their Saviour. We need men of God who will preach the truth from their pulpits and not be concerned with what is popular among their people and even among society. This generation is dying for men of God who will stop trying to become popular among society and among the news media and realize there is a greater need in our nation. There is a need for men of God like Elijah who will do right even if they are the only one who will stand. Far too many preachers will only do what the populace says to do so that they can be accepted among their peers. Because of this, they are allowing their movement to be destroyed. They are more concerned with what their alma mater says than with what their God says. May I say, if this generation of preachers continues this then this generation of preachers will lead their nation to the judgment of God. Oh, for a people who will learn to stand alone. It is not easy to stand alone, but it is the right thing to do if the crowd is not doing right.

2. He knew how to live by faith.

We have the story in **1 Kings 17:8-16** about Elijah going to the widow woman of Zarephath to ask her to make a meal for

153

him to eat. It was during this time that the famine that he had prophesied was in full swing and food was beginning to become a precious commodity in the land because of the lack of it. Here this widow woman was gathering a few sticks to start a fire so she could make the last meal for her and her son to eat and then they would starve to death if a miracle did not happen. Elijah came and asked her to give him the food. She informed him of her lack of food, but still made him the meal though she knew she was giving the last meal, that she and her son would eat to the man of God. What faith this took for this dear lady and what faith this took for Elijah. It was by faith that Elijah believed that God would take care of him and this widow woman as He said He would. Yes, Elijah was a man who lived by faith, and it was this faith that God saw in Elijah years prior to God promoting him to prominence.

The Bible says in **Hebrews 11:6, "But without faith it is impossible to please him: for he that cometh to God must believe that he is, and that he is a rewarder of them that diligently seek him."** Any person who will be used of God in a great way will have to learn to live by faith. Every man of God who has become a great man of God first learned to live by faith. Why? Because it is only by faith and living by faith that we get the attention of God and please God.

We live in a society that knows nothing about living by faith. The average young person today has been raised in a home where mom and dad pay for everything they do. If they ever had to live by faith, God pity them, for they would probably starve to death. You will find very few people who know what living by faith is all about. It used to be talked about all the time. Men of God would stand in their pulpits and would tell stories of how they lived by faith and God would supply their needs. It was this faith that raised up a great generation of men of God. Yet, go to the average Bible College today and try to get a young person to go out and live by faith and you will find that this is next to impossible. I taught at a Bible college for several years, and truthfully, the one thing that was hard to find was young people who were willing to live by faith.

154

Their parents bought their cars and paid their tuition, and then we wonder why we can't get these same young people to take a position in a church that would require them to live by faith. Instead, these young people only take positions where they know they can live comfortably. God will never bless people like this.

I was raised in a family that lived by faith most of my childhood years. My father, who was a preacher, never pastored a large church and never had a large salary. Many times we would literally have to pray down food in order to have something to eat. If it wasn't for the kindnesses of people bringing over bags of groceries in needy times, we would not have had anything to eat. Yet, this is how God takes care of you when you live by faith. It was this type of upbringing that gave me the faith to step out into full-time evangelism many years ago. I remember when I stepped out in evangelism, I only had four meetings on my calendar, but I was determined to do what God called me to do. That first year in evangelism I made a total of four thousand dollars. You say how did you make it on four thousand dollars? I made it by living by faith! Unless you are willing to live by faith, God will never use you in a great way. Parents, stop paying the way for your children and make them learn to live by faith. If they don't learn to live by faith and pray down their needs, then what are they going to do when you are gone? No great man of God and no great Christian has ever become great in the spiritual realm without learning to live by faith. This is one of the great qualities that we find in the life of the prophet Elijah. He was a man that lived by faith.

3. He lived a simple lifestyle.

I know this may seem redundant to some who may read this book, but may I say that when you study the great men of God in the Bible, you will find that many of them lived simple lifestyles. This was the case with Elijah as we read in **2 Kings 1:8**, **"And they answered him, He was an hairy man, and girt with a girdle of leather about his loins. And he said, It**

155

is Elijah the Tishbite." Elijah was not a man of fancy clothing, he was not a man who rode around in fancy chariots, and he was not a man who frequented the high priced restaurants of his day. No, Elijah was a man who knew how to live a simple lifestyle.

Compare how Elijah lived to the average, so called preacher of today. As you look at the prosperity gospel preachers who promote their lavish lifestyles wearing all the fancy clothing and flaunting the money that they have prostituted from sincere, hard-working, and honest people, you wonder how they would even stand up to a great man of God like Elijah. Now please do not get me wrong as I make some of these statements, I do not think it is sinful to enjoy some of the pleasures of life. I do not think it is wrong when preachers wear nice clothing. What I am trying to get across is the fact that men of God and Christians alike need to get back to living simple lifestyles and stop trying to impress everyone with what they have. Trust me, God is not impressed with where you buy your clothes and God is not impressed with the car that you drive. Do you think that God cannot afford these things? One of my biggest concerns for our generation is that we have lost the value of living simply. We are more concerned with trying to impress everyone else with our fancy clothing, our padded bank accounts, fancy cars and houses than we are about impressing God with a spiritual heart. We should be more concerned with pleasing God than with living a fancy lifestyle. Now I think men of God ought to dress as sharp as they can and I believe Christians ought to look sharp in their appearance, but what we need to get back to is learning how to live simple lives and give more of our attention to helping others than trying to impress others with what we have. We need to learn to stop trying to live extravagantly and learn to live like the common man. It is the common man that most of us are going to reach, and we will never reach them when we live above them. When the common man sees that we know how to live simply like they do and yet we still serve God, then maybe the common man will want to listen to us.

4. He lived up to his name.

The name Elijah means "my God is Jehovah." Elijah most
certainly lived up to the meaning of his name. Elijah lived a
life that proved that his God was Jehovah God. You look at
the miracles that God performed through his life and look at
how he relied completely upon God throughout his life, and
you will see that Elijah lived his life as if his God was Jehovah.
He did not live a life that was in direct contradiction to the
meaning of his name, and he did not live a life that would tear
down the testimony that he had. He lived a life above
reproach and carried the testimony that he was a man of God
whose God was Jehovah.

Likewise, we also should live up to the name of a Christian. If
you are a Christian then that is the name that you have been
given and you ought to live a life that is becoming of a
Christian, which is being like Christ. Now when I say
Christian, I am talking about a person that has accepted
Jesus Christ as their personal Saviour and does not trust their
works, their baptism, church membership, or anything else, to
take them to Heaven. Now when you get saved, you become
a Christian and you should live up to this great name.
Christian, don't live a life that will bring a reproach to the name
Christian. Live in such a way that the name Christian is
exalted because of your testimony! Live your life above
reproach so that no one can point their finger at you and say
that you have not lived up to the name of a Christian.

5. He let truth influence him, not crowds and position.

Now truthfully, I need not spend much time on this point as we
have already covered this earlier in this chapter, but let me
just once again reinforce this point. Elijah allowed truth to be
the major influence of his actions and not the crowds and
positions that he could obtain from man. In **1 Kings 18:22**
you will remember that he stood up to the four hundred false
prophets of Baal because of truth and for the sake of keeping
truth alive in his generation.

The determining thing that influences any one of us ought to be truth. Truth should always be the thing that determines what we are going to do, what we are going to say and where we are going to go. We should not let what the crowd is doing or some position that we could hold if we will just let up on truth entice us. Far too many people in life are concerned with the position on their job than they are about living for truth. Listen, if you must compromise truth to acquire position on the job or even in society, then forsake the position and stand for truth. We as Christians need to realize the life that we live is a short life and one day we will live forever in a place called Heaven. We should live in this world as if our final destination is Heaven and not earth. I see too many church members who will let up on their dress standards and even on their church attendance for the sake of getting along with the crowds. May I say, truth is far more important than what the crowds want you to do. Never be guilty of forsaking truth for the sake of what is popular with the crowds and for the sake of gaining a higher position among the world. Truth should always be the factor that decides ultimately what we are going to do. When truth becomes this important to you then God can use you, because God can use a person who makes truth their ultimate decision maker in life.

6. He was not afraid to put God to the test.

In **1 Kings 18:22-24** Elijah puts God to the test by challenging the false prophets of Baal to a contest to see which God could send fire down from Heaven. The God that did do this would be the God of Israel. Now to be quite honest with you, this took some backbone and some faith in God for Elijah to make this challenge. Never before had he seen God send fire from Heaven and never before had he even read about this. And yet, he put God to the test because he just believed that God is the God of the impossible. Not only did he make this challenge, but when it came time for him to pray fire down from Heaven, he had some young men pour a total of twelve barrels of water on the altar before he started praying. I don't know how much water those barrels held, but conservatively, if those barrels only held one gallon of water, that would mean twelve gallons of water was poured on the altar. Now lets just be quite frank with each other, this seemed to be quite ludicrous for him to do this, and even seemed to make the task more difficult for God. Yet Elijah was a man who was not afraid to put his God to the test and prove to the world that he served the all powerful God. As we read the rest of the story we see that Elijah did pray fire down from Heaven, and God came through as He always does when you put Him to the test.

Let me remind you of a verse in **2 Chronicles 16:9** where it says, **"For the eyes of the LORD run to and fro throughout the whole earth, to shew himself strong in the behalf of them whose heart is perfect toward him."** God is consistently looking for a person or individual who is willing to show this world that God is the God of the impossible and for someone who is willing to let God show His power through them. People who have been greatly used by God have put God to the test. Just look at some of the stories of great people in the Bible. Moses put God to the test by asking God to part the great Red Sea. Gideon put God to the test by having only three hundred men who went against the great Midianite army whose number was as the sand of the sea. David put God to the test by fighting the great giant Goliath with just a sling and a stone. Joshua put God to the test by asking God to knock down the walls of Jericho. Time and time again great people of the Bible were not afraid to put God to the test, and the amazing thing was that God always came through for them. Yes, God told them in many cases that He wanted them to do something that truthfully seemed impossible, but it took their faith to put their God to the test to see if He would come through.

Great Christians and great men of God are people who put their God to the test and prove to the world that God still uses man to do His great work. Let me ask you, when is the last time you put God to the test? Have you not done it because

159

you are so afraid that He just won't come through for you? Well, let me just tell you, it takes faith to put God to the test, but God always honors a person's faith when they have a sincere heart and want to show to the world that He is still God. I believe that one of the biggest reasons we do not see the miracles of God like we read about in the Bible is because we limit what God can do through our faithlessness. Our lack of faith keeps God from proving His power. If you plan on being used in a great way by God then you are going to have to learn to step out and put God to the test. If you are going to be used of God, you are going to have to be willing to put your name on the chopping block in society and trust God.

7. He was a man of order.

Notice in **1 Kings 18:33** that the false prophets of Baal had knocked down the altar and now Elijah begins to **"...put the wood in order..."** Elijah was not a man who did things haphazardly; he was a man who believed in doing things in their proper order. As insignificant as this may seem, it is important to God that everything is done in the right way and everything is done in proper order. This is why Elijah put the wood back in order. He knew his God was a God of order, and if God was going to use him then he must be a man of order.

Very rarely will you ever find a person who is being used in a great way that is highly unorganized in life. I had the privilege for several years to be under the ministry of Dr. Jack Hyles who pastored the great First Baptist Church of Hammond, Indiana. For many years I was a member of his church. For many years my ministry was out of his church and for several years I represented the college that he started, Hyles-Anderson College. Through all that time I learned one thing about this great man of God; he was a very organized man and believed in things being done in order. Even now as my ministry is under the leadership of Dr. Jeff Owens who pastors the Shenandoah Bible Baptist Church in Martinsburg, West Virginia, I see that he is a very organized man who also

160

believes in everything being done in its proper order. Maybe this is one of the reasons why God has blessed our church in such a great way. If you study the great men of God of the past who were used by God in a great way you will see that these men were men of order. Don't fool yourself into thinking that the day of Pentecost in the Bible, where three thousand people were saved and baptized, just happened without any order. I promise you they had to organize and plan and everything was done in order.

I believe our God is a God of order. All you have to do is go to the book of Genesis and see the order in which God set this world, and you will come to realize that God is a God of order. Any great person who is used by God will have to become a person who believes in order. When you spend time with God, God will rub off on you and will make you a person of order. Just recently my wife was relaying to me a conversation that she had with my sister. My sister asked her if I still pack everything in my suitcase in a certain order. I love what my wife said when she responded to my sister. My wife told her she should know that I have always been a person of order. You see, I just believe that if God is going to use anyone, they are going to have to learn how to organize their lives. Organize your daytime by living by a schedule. Organize your finances by living by a budget. Organize your family by keeping the proper roles of authority in your home. Anything that is ever going to be used by God must have order to it, **"For God is not the author of confusion..."**, as 1 Corinthians 14:33 says. God is a God of order.

8. He learned the value of proper rest.

I want you to notice how I worded this point. I said that Elijah learned the value of proper rest, meaning that he did not immediately understand this. Let me explain by telling you the story in **1 Kings 19:8-18**. Elijah had just won the challenge to the false prophets of Baal and had even slain all four hundred of these prophets. But Jezebel, the wicked wife of King Ahab, had now put a bounty on the head of Elijah. At the hearing of

161

this, he ran for his life. We see him in this tired state of mind becoming discouraged and beginning to lack some of the great faith that he had exemplified in the past. He even came to the point of life when he just wanted God to kill him. This was nothing more than Elijah wanting to quit. Now what drove Elijah to this point? Very simply put, he had become very tired. Yet notice what God did in this story, God allowed Elijah to get some well-needed rest to recharge his spiritual batteries so he could go back and preach the truths of God again. I believe that Elijah learned a very valuable lesson. He learned the importance of getting the proper rest so that he does not allow himself to become so weak physically that he becomes discouraged and loses faith.

I am a person who loves to work and who also rises early in the morning. However, I also believe that it is important to get the proper rest so that you can serve God to your fullest potential. Without the proper rest you are opening yourself up to discouragement and temptation. When you are tired, you have less strength to fight the temptations that Satan will throw at you, and believe me, he knows that you are more susceptible to temptation when you are tired. Even our Saviour Jesus Christ, when living in an earthly body down here on this earth, took time to rest. Now if Jesus took time to rest, I would think we should understand the importance of resting our bodies. There is nothing spiritual about going without rest. I know people who brag all the time about how little rest they get and this is foolish. The only thing they are doing is setting themselves up for temptation, and if they don't succumb to temptation their bodies will succumb to sickness. We can all serve God better with proper rest! I am not talking about loving to sleep, but I am talking about sleeping so you can live and serve God the way that you should. Be sure that you get the proper rest so that you can serve God to your fullest potential.

9. He knew how to fight discouragement.

Notice Elijah is now trying to fight discouragement and we see in **1 Kings 19:19** that the way he fought discouragement was to invest his life in the lives of others. In this case, it was a young man by the name of Elisha.

You fight discouragement by investing your life in the lives of others. Discouragement is you keeping your eyes on yourself and how you are treated. This will only lead to more discouragement. The quickest way out of discouragement is to go out and invest your life in others. You will find this truly is the quickest way to fight discouragement. People who are used by God in a great way are people who know how to overcome discouragement very quickly. I don't know a person alive who has never been discouraged at some time in their life, but those who do great things for God are people who learn how to get out of that discouraging state. The way they do this is by helping others. You see, when you help others you take your eyes off of yourself and this will most certainly lift your spirits. If you want to be used by God in a great way then you must learn how to overcome discouragement quickly. We have learned through the life of Elijah that the best way to do this is to go out and help others.

10. He was an encourager to other men of God.

Elijah's life was certainly an encouragement to other men of God who were wondering if anyone else out there was standing up for God. In **I Kings 20:28** we read about another man of God who begins to stand up to the wicked king and prophesy to King Ahab. I believe that it was because of the life of Elijah that other men of God were encouraged to do what was right. You will notice just a couple of chapters earlier that Elijah was saying that he was the only one who was willing to stand up against the four hundred false prophets of Baal, and then later in chapter nineteen God reminds Elijah of seven thousand other men of God who had not bowed the knee to Baal. I believe that one of the seven thousand is talked about in this verse. Elijah never knew the influence that his life had on other men of God. His life of standing for truth began to embolden other men of God to come out and do what was right.

You will notice the lives of those whom God uses always embolden others to take a stand for right. Now why is this? He was not afraid to stand alone, and by standing alone he encouraged others to do right. We need to understand that as hard as it may be to stand for right, our standing for right will always encourage others to do right. When you stand for right on the job, other Christians will receive strength from you to stand up for right. When you stand for right in school or college, other Christians will be encouraged to stand up for what is right. When you stand for right in your country, your stand for right will encourage other Christians to stand for right in their country. Great Christians just learn to stand for right and that stand always encourages those who do not have the courage to stand up for right alone. Now it may be lonely for awhile, but if you will just stick with it, you will see the fruits of your standing as Elijah did just a few chapters after his stand.

11. He prepared others to take his place.

Maybe one of the greatest things that Elijah did in his life was when he, in **1 Kings 19:19**, laid his mantle upon the young man Elisha. What was Elijah doing by laying his mantle upon him? He was preparing Elisha to take his place when he was gone. He knew that he was not going to be around forever. If what he had stood for all of these years, and what he had strived to build all of those years was going to continue, then he must prepare someone else to carry on in his place once he was gone.

One of the great traits of great leaders is when they are not afraid to train others to do what they have done in their lifetime. Great Christians will realize that they are not going to live forever, and they must be sure to prepare others to take their place once they are gone. I am talking about Sunday school teachers who need to realize that their job is to train others to take their place when they are gone. Even bus workers and bus captains should train others how to run a bus route because one day when they are gone, if they want that bus route to continue, they need to have trained someone else to run that route. Even preachers need to be like Elijah in that they need to start training several young men to pastor their church. One day someone will have to pastor that church, and if you have not trained someone, then who is going to take that church to new heights for the glory of God? Anyone who has a position should learn to train others to take their position so that when the day comes when they go to Heaven, those whom they have trained can take their place and carry on what they have worked for all those years.

12. He lived to please God with his life.

I cannot say a better thing about the life of Elijah than that his whole life was about one thing, trying to please God. In **Hebrews 11:5** it says, **"By faith Enoch was translated that he should not see death; and was not found, because God had translated him: for before his translation he had this testimony, that he pleased God."** That word "pleased" in this verse means he made God happy. He lived his life to make God happy. The result of this was that God translated him from this earth to Heaven so that he would not have to see death.

If a person will live their life to try to please God, I promise you, God will translate their life or change their life into a life that is worthy of being used. God wanted to use Elijah because he lived his life to please Him. I don't know what you need to change in your life, but whatever you need to change in your life, you will only change it by trying to please God and make God happy with your life. You see, when you try to make God happy, you will realize that you must stop doing some of the things that cause God not to be happy: sin. Time and space would not allow me to start naming all of the sin, but I am confident that most everyone knows what is right and

165

what is wrong. Those who live to make God happy and pleased will lay aside the sin and filth in their lives to live a life that is righteous and holy. This is pleasing in the eyes of God. This desire alone will translate or change your life. Any person who has a desire to be used by God in a great way must decide to live their whole life to please God and not to please themselves and their selfish desires.

Elijah most certainly was a great man of God! Thank God for the testimony and the lessons that we can read about and learn from the life of Elijah. Now why don't you take these lessons and apply them to your life and see if God can use you in a great way like he did Elijah? It does not matter if you are not a person of reputation or great background, it only matters that you live to please God and do what He wants you to do. When you do this, God will most likely see fit to use you in a greater way just like He did Elijah.

12

Picking Up the Mantle

2 Kings 2:12-14, "And Elisha saw it, and he cried, My father, my father, the chariot of Israel, and the horsemen thereof. And he saw him no more: and he took hold of his own clothes, and rent them in two pieces. He took up also the mantle of Elijah that fell from him, and went back and stood by the bank of Jordan; And he took the mantle of Elijah that fell from him, and smote the waters, and said, Where is the LORD God of Elijah? and when he also had smitten the waters, they parted hither and thither: and Elisha went over."

There is a group of people in Christianity who, I believe more than any other group, have the greatest chance to do something great for God. That group is those who we call second-generation Christians. A second-generation Christian is someone who has grown up in church and has never lived in the world. They were saved as a child and grew up in church. The second-generation Christian has lived in a good home with both parents who have brought their children to church their whole lives. They were not saved out of a life of wickedness and probably have never known many of the vices that their mom and dad have known. To them, Christianity is second nature. It is just as natural to them to live the Christian life as it is for people to eat and sleep every day. The Christian life is all this generation has known.

I am a part of this generation. When the Psalmist says in **Psalms 16:6, "...I have a goodly heritage..."**, certainly I can concur with this statement. As far as I know, I am a sixth-generation preacher. My dad was a preacher and my parents raised me in church. I like to say I went to church nine months before I was born because my mother was involved in church while I was in her womb. The truth is, I have no excuse to give if I ever mess up my life because I was raised in church and I am a part of the second-generation of Christians.

If any group ought to do more for God it should be the second-generation Christians. You see, this generation has all of the experience of the first generation. The second-generation Christian should have learned from all the experiences of the first generation. On top of this, the first generation most likely has taught the second generation the wisdom that they have learned in their lifetime. So, by the time the second generation turns eighteen years of age, they should have learned all the wisdom of their parents and applied this wisdom to their lives. Yes, this second generation should do more for God than the first generation because of the background they have. They should do twice as much as the first generation. They have a head start on the first generation because of the experience and wisdom they should have learned from that first generation. Yet the truth is, in the majority of cases, this just does not happen. Most of the time the first generation Christians end up doing more for God than the second generation. What a shame and what an indictment to the second generation when they have been given such a heritage to carry on.

Elisha was a part of this second generation of Christians. Let me explain by telling you a little about his life. When Elijah came to call on Elisha, he found him plowing in the field. The preacher came to him and told him to come and follow him. I believe that certainly the parents of Elisha had raised him right. Elisha was raised in church. As Elisha started following the great man of God, Elijah, we see that everywhere the preacher went Elisha was right there by his side learning from the man of God. The day came when Elijah was to be taken up to Heaven. I don't know how, but apparently God had told Elijah that He was going to take him up to Heaven on that day. As they journeyed to the location where God would take up Elijah, Elijah four different times had asked Elisha to stay in each place as he would journey to where God would take him up to Heaven. Elisha told the preacher he was not going to leave his side and that he would go with him until he was taken up to Heaven. Finally, Elijah asked Elisha what he could do for him. Elisha's response was to ask for a double portion of Elijah's spirit. The promise was given that if he saw him taken up to Heaven then he would receive this request. The time came, the chariot from Heaven had come and Elijah stepped inside the chariot and rode up to Heaven. Elisha seeing this, and seeing the leather mantle of Elijah fall to the earth, went over and picked up this mantle and filled the position that Elijah's vacancy had left. As we study the life of Elisha we see that in his lifetime he ended up doing twice as much as Elijah had done. Now I don't know that this makes him a greater prophet. He should have done twice as much because he was a second-generation Christian. I don't know which of these men was greater, I just know that Elisha did what every second-generation Christian should do; they should do twice as much for God as the first generation did.

If the second-generation Christian is going to do what Elisha did in doing twice as much for God as the previous generation, then we need to learn what kind of life he lived in order for us to have the same results that he had. If we are going to pick up the mantle of the first generation and get the blessings of God upon us like Elisha did, then let us learn what made him into this man. Let us copy what he has done so we can see the same great results in our lives that Elisha did.

1. He wasn't afraid to get dirty.

In **1 Kings 19:19** we see when Elijah came to call Elisha to follow him, Elisha was plowing in the field with the yoke of oxen. Elisha was most certainly a hard worker, for farm work is not easy. But beyond him being a hard worker, he also realized that he was not too good to get his hands dirty.

169

How important it is for the second-generation Christian to realize that they are never too good to get their hands dirty. I have watched generations of Christians who have grown up in church think that they are above some of the work in the church because of who their parents are. May I say this is wrong and nobody is too good to do any work in the church. The second generation should have to work their way up the ladder just like the first-generation Christian did. We should not just give positions to them; we should make them earn their positions just like everyone else has had to earn their position. I can remember when I was a boy growing up, many times my dad would have me clean the toilets in the church, pull the weeds in the flower beds or even vacuum the church floors on Saturday before the Sunday services. My dad never allowed me to think that I was above any job in the church. How the second-generation Christian needs to learn to not be afraid to get their hands dirty. This type of mentality is where you earn the respect of the first generation.

A few summers ago we had a leak in the roof of our house and after getting a few repair bids, I decided I could do the work myself. I called up my wife's uncle who was a professional roofer his entire life and asked him if he would come and help me put the roof on my house if I paid him. He and his wife came and for three days in the hot West Virginia summer, he and I were on the roof putting shingles down. After those days were over he commented to his wife that he enjoyed working with me and that he was happy to see how hard I had worked. You see, all he had known of me was that I was a preacher, and to him most preachers were not the hardest of workers. He had been a hard worker his entire life and one of the easiest ways to gain his respect was to be a hard worker. After spending those days with me on the roof and seeing that I was not afraid to get my hands dirty, I had gained a new respect from him that I would have never gained had I been afraid to get my hands dirty.

Every second-generation Christian needs to learn and realize that they are never above any job. They need to realize if they are going to do twice as much as the previous generation then they need to gain the respect of those watching them. The way to gain that respect is through hard work and not being afraid to get their hands dirty.

2. He made sure he left right.

After Elijah had told Elisha to come and follow him, Elisha asked the preacher in **1 Kings 19:20**, to allow him to go back and kiss his parents goodbye. Elisha was a man who knew the importance of leaving right whenever he left. He realized as a second-generation Christian you have one opportunity to leave a place correctly, so he had better do it right the first time.

I believe it is so important for the second-generation Christian to learn to leave in the proper way. When you leave home, you need to make sure that you leave your parents in the right way. Don't leave your parents under bad circumstances. Be sure when you leave home that you and your parents have a good relationship. Listen, you only have one set of parents, and though they may not always be perfect, they are still your parents. You need to make sure that when you leave home, your parents know that you love them. How important it is for the second generation of Christians to learn to say "I love you" to their parents! How important it is for this generation to learn to hug and kiss their parents before leaving. I know, you say that you are just not the hugging and kissing type. Well let me say to you, become that type, for one day you will not have your parents to hug and kiss. It is so vitally important to learn to leave home the right way.

Not only should you learn to leave home the right way, but you should also learn to leave your church the right way. When leaving your church, be sure to leave under the right conditions and not under conditions of adversity. Be sure that when you leave your church you leave those who are in that church with a good taste of you. If for some reason you must leave a church under adverse conditions, then let me just say that first of all you need to make sure that you are right with God and that you are not leaving over personality conflicts. If for some reason you find yourself having to leave a church because you disagree with what is going on in the church, then leave quietly. You have no right to leave that church and make a big stink as you leave and make everyone else think that you are some super Christian. The truth is, if you leave under these conditions then the people of the church should not know why you are leaving. Always be careful to leave in the right way, because it is hard to get the blessings of God upon you if you leave the wrong way.

3. He had a love for his parents.

Again in **1 Kings 19:20** you see Elisha say, **"...Let me, I pray thee, kiss my father and my mother, and then I will follow thee."** Certainly for Elisha to want to go back and kiss his parents tells us that he loved his parents dearly. If he thought it was important to go back and kiss his parents before leaving then I would think that he loved his parents. He would not have done this if he did not love his parents.

I won't spend as much time on this as I have previously, yet, let me say to the second-generation Christian, don't think that you are too good for your parents because of how you were raised. Don't get the mentality that because you have not done some of the things that your parents did that you are better than them. God does not bless those who do not honor their parents. Just because your parents did some things that you have not done does not make you better than them. They probably did not have the same upbringing that you have had. You shouldn't have done some of the things that they have done. You should have a cleaner life than what they have had because you had a better opportunity to live right than they did. Don't hold over their heads that they did some things that you have not done. Instead, you should be thankful that they raised you in such a way that you did not have to experience some of the sin that your parents have.

In addition to this, let me also say that you should not hold against your parents how hard your upbringing was. Far too many second-generation Christians complain about how hard their parents were on them. Some are almost to the point where they hold a grudge against them for the hard times that they had to go through as a child. Listen, the hard times that your parents raised you in have made you the person that you are. Instead of complaining about those hard times, you should be thanking your parents that they loved you enough to teach you how to make it through the hard times of life, for those hard times made you. Every second-generation Christian should love their parents by living right and by doing what they raised you to do. Don't try to prove them wrong by living a different life than what they raised you to live just to show that you are right. Instead, show your love to your parents by living the way they raised you to live.

4. He didn't seek position; he sought to help others.

Notice in **1 Kings 19:21** that it says, **"Then he arose, and went after Elijah, and ministered unto him."** Elisha was not a man who was seeking position in life; instead he was a man who sought to live his life trying to help others. He followed the man of God with one purpose in mind, and this was to meet the needs of the preacher.

How this generation needs a good dose of this again! We live in a society that is constantly trying to jockey for position and everything we do is all about trying to get position. Whatever happened to the days when everything we do is done for the sake of helping others with no ulterior motives in mind? How important it is for a generation of people to learn that we should not be doing things just to get position, we should do things for the sake of helping others.

5. He did his best to help the man of God.

Referring back to **1 Kings 19:21**, we see Elisha spending his life trying his best to be a help to the man of God. Whatever

173

needs he found the man of God had, he tried everything in his power to meet those needs.

If the second generation of Christians is going to do twice as much as the first generation, then the second-generation Christian needs to start trying to be a help to the man of God. You ought not to be a headache to your preacher, but you ought to try to be a help to your preacher. Don't be guilty of being the one whom the preacher is concerned with because you are rebelling against what your parents are teaching you. Don't be the one who is guilty of putting the preacher in a premature grave because of the lifestyle that you are living. Instead, find ways to be a help to the preacher. I would advise every second-generation Christian to find themselves constantly following the man of God, trying to seek out the needs that he has and then do what you can to help meet those needs. You may not have the money to meet the needs of the man of God, but you can certainly get involved in the church and help the man of God in the church. No doubt you can help the man of God by cleaning up the church auditorium or by helping him with the cleaning up of the church yard. There are so many duties in the church that the preacher has to do that certainly any person, if they look hard enough, can find something with which to help the man of God. You can help the man of God by getting involved in the church. You can help the man of God by inviting people to church. You can help the man of God by listening and responding when he is preaching. You can help the man of God by writing him encouraging notes. There are so many ways you can be a help to the man of God. Determine as a second-generation Christian that you are going to be the type of person who is a help to the man of God.

6. He lived a separated life.

We read in **2 Kings 2:1** that Elijah is about ready to be taken up to Heaven. As they journey, the Bible says that **"...Elijah went with Elisha from Gilgal."** Now I want you to notice that it says that Elijah went with Elisha, not Elisha went with Elijah.

174

Notice where they were coming from: they were coming from a city called Gilgal. This city was the place where the children of Israel first set up camp after crossing over the Jordan River. Gilgal was a type of separation from the world, as it symbolized the leaving of the wilderness to go into the Promised Land. Elisha lived a separated life! Elijah had to go to Gilgal to get Elisha, for he was already living a life of separation.

How important this is for people to realize that if we are going to have a double portion of the blessings of God on our lives then we are going to have to live separated lives to get that double portion. I am talking about being separated from the world. I mean, we ought to be separated from the world's dress, from the world's music and even from the world's friends. God cannot bless people who are not separated from the world. We should not be trying to be like the world, but instead we should be trying to be separated from the world and be like God. Not only should we live a separated life from the world, but we should also live a separated life from those who are backslidden. We need to be careful about running with the crowd that is backslidden and learn that if we are going to have God's blessings upon us, then we need to learn to live separated lives from those who are not living for God. Now I am not saying that we should be rude to these people. I think we ought to be kind and courteous to these people when we see them. What I am saying is we ought not to be going to functions with people who are of the world and are backslidden. God blesses separated people. Until we become separate from the world, then it will be hard for them to see a difference in our lives so that we can be a help to them.

7. He made the house of God important.

1 Kings 2:2 says, **"So they went down to Bethel."** Bethel, in the Bible, is always a type of the house of God. Elisha knew the importance of spending time in the house of God. This is part of what made him the man that he was. This is part of the reason that God used him in the way that he did because Elisha knew the importance of being in the house of God.

Likewise every Christian, especially the second-generation Christian, needs to understand the importance of the house of God. God will not bless those second-generation Christians who do not make the house of God important to them. Stop thinking that your "spirituality" gives you a right to miss church! It matters not how long you have been saved and how long you have gone to church, God's house is still important. I have seen far too many second-generation Christians think that because they have gone to church all these years, missing a few services here and there is not a problem with God. Well let me just inform you, it is a problem with God for He says in **Hebrews 10:25, "...Not forsaking the assembling of ourselves together..."** God does not look at how long you have gone to church and then give you a pass for missing church because of your past attendance record. No, every Christian who aspires to be used of God in a great way must make the house of God important to them.

8. He learned the importance of personally having great victories.

In **2 Kings 2:4**, we see Elisha and Elijah leaving Bethel to go down to Jericho. Jericho is known as the place of great victories. It was the place where Israel crossed over on dry land to go into the Promised Land. Elisha learned very early in his life that he could not rely on the victories of Elijah, but that he needed God to give him victories also.

Second-generation Christians cannot rely on their parents or preacher's victories. They must learn to pray down great victories for themselves. You cannot just think that the victories of mom and dad and the preacher are good enough for you. Every second-generation Christian must get their own answers to prayer. I can remember growing up hearing of all the victories of my parents and of the guest preachers

176

who came to preach in our church, but I realized very early in my ministry that I needed to learn to pray down those same victories for myself. The reason for this is that we need to learn that we have the same God that the previous generation has and that this God still has the power to do for us what He has done for them. Let me just ask you as you read this book, when is the last time you prayed down a great victory in your life? Are you depending upon the victories of previous generations to get you through the Christian life? If you are going to be used in a great way and do twice as much as the previous generation, then you are going to have to learn to pray down victories for yourself and not rely on the victories of the past generations.

9. He desired God's power more than the crowd's acceptance.

As Elisha is following Elijah on the last day that Elijah was on this earth, we see in **2 Kings 2:1-8**, that there are several other preacher boys following and almost trying to discourage him from following Elijah. But Elisha knew one thing; if he would just stay with Elijah then he would eventually get the power of God upon him as Elijah promised. To Elisha, the power of God was more important to him than having the acceptance of the crowd.

Until you get to the point in your life where God's power means more to you than being accepted by the crowd, you will never get God's power. You will always find in the Bible that God's power comes on individuals and not on crowds. It is always interesting that as long as they were with the crowds they did not get God's power. God's power comes on an individual who learns to get away from the crowd and get alone with God. Unless you learn to get alone with God and unless you learn that you must leave the crowd to spend time alone with God, you will never experience the power of God upon your life. How this nation needs second-generation Christians to stop being concerned with the acceptance of the crowd and learn to get alone and walk with God alone so that they can receive God's power on their lives. Until this happens, they can be guaranteed that they will not do twice as much as the first generation, because this is how the first generation received God's power on their lives: through spending time alone with God.

10. He stood with the man of God when other stood afar off.

Notice in **2 Kings 2:7**, you will read that the fifty sons of the prophets went, but the Bible says that they **"...stood to view afar off..."** Elisha knew the importance of being close to the man of God. These other men had the right direction but they had the wrong distance.

Your distance to the man of God shows your heart for God. You show me what you think about your preacher, and I will show you what you think about your God. You show me how much time you desire to be around your preacher, and again, I will show you how much time you want to be around God. There are many people out there who are just like these fifty sons of the prophets who have a right direction but the wrong distance from the preacher. I not only want to be going the right direction with the man of God, but I also want to have the right distance from the man of God, and that is close by his side. I am talking about people who, instead of sitting up close in church, always want to sit in the back of the church. They never want to be too close to the man of God; they only want to stand afar off. I am reminded of the Apostle Peter who did the same thing with our Saviour, in that he stood afar off. Peter had the right direction but the wrong distance, and that wrong distance caused him to end up warming his hands at the heathen's fire. Likewise, the same will happen to those who follow the man of God at the wrong distance. They will soon find themselves warming their hands at the heathen's fire and soon find themselves out of church. If we are going to pick up the mantle of the man of God, then we need to be close enough so that when the mantle falls, we can pick it up. Those who follow afar off are never there to pick up the

178

mantle. Such is the case with this world today: far too many Christians have followed afar off, and when the mantle fell, there was no one there to pick up the mantle. Let us find ourselves close to the man of God so that we can pick up that mantle when it falls.

11. He did not want to be average.

How I love this about Elisha! When Elijah asked Elisha what he could do for him, Elisha responded in **2 Kings 2:9, "...I pray thee, let a double portion of thy spirit be upon me."** Elisha said, "I don't want just a single portion of your spirit but I want a double portion of your spirit." What was Elisha saying? He was saying that he did not want to be like everyone else and just be average. He was saying he wanted to go beyond the average.

Oh, how I long for every Christian to get this type of desire inside of them, especially the second generation Christian. We need Christians to stop being satisfied with being like everyone else and start trying to be the best and do more than those before us. My whole life this has been my desire. I have never wanted to be just an average Christian. I have never wanted to be just an average soul winner. I have never wanted to be just an average preacher. Many of my prayers to God have been filled with the request that God would not allow me to be average. I constantly beg God for a double portion in my life. I have told God over and over again, that if I am just going to be average that I would rather Him take me to Heaven. I don't want to be an average person! I have grown up in church and seen too many Christians happy with being the average. No wonder our nation is in the shape that she is in. No nation will ever be turned around for God with a bunch of average Christians. Look at those in the Bible whom God used to do great things: they were not average; they were above average. Everyday of my life I ask God to give me a double portion of answered prayers, a double portion of His wisdom, His Joy, His love and His power. I don't want to just be average, and my hope and prayer is that you don't

179

want to just be average. If second-generation Christians are going to do anything great for God, then they cannot be satisfied with a single portion. They must strive for and ask for a double portion from God. They must live their lives to be above average.

12. He was not afraid to copy great men.

You will notice in **2 Kings 2:14**, Elijah is gone and now Elisha has picked up the mantle and gone back to the Jordan River. As he approaches the river the Bible says, **"...he took the mantle of Elijah that fell from him, and smote the waters, and said, Where is the LORD God of Elijah? and when he also had smitten the waters, they parted hither and thither: and Elisha went over."** What was Elisha doing? He was simply copying what Elijah had done to part the Jordan River. Elisha was not afraid to copy the man of God. He realized that if it worked for Elijah then he would be wise to simply copy what Elijah had done. He did not try to put a new niche on how it was done; he simply copied the success of the great man of God.

We must all realize that every one of us is a copy of several individuals in our lives. None of us are our "own person". I get so tired of hearing people say, "I am my own man" as if that makes them something great. The truth is nobody is "their own man". All of us have simply copied different people who have had an influence on our lives. I am never ashamed to tell people that I am a copy. I have learned in my life that if something has worked for someone else, if I copy that, most likely I will also be successful in that same endeavor. To those who have heard me preach, they will know one thing if they knew my preacher, this is that my preaching is a copy of successful preachers of the past. Many times when I preach people will come to me and tell me that I remind them of some great man of God who they have heard in the past. How honored I am when they say this. To be identified with a great man of God is nothing but a great honor. It does not offend me, for I know that I am a copy. I have studied these men

180

and how they preach and have copied that which caught my attention. I realized that if it caught my attention then it will catch the attention of those to whom I preach. Never be afraid to copy the great Christians of the past. If you are a copy of them, then most certainly you will be a great Christian in your own way. This is truthfully all that a Christian is, a copy of Christ!

13. He understood the importance of his position.

In **2 Kings 2:23-24** we have the story of some young boys making fun of Elisha and mocking him by calling him a bald man. Now I know we have used these verses in jest many a time, but there is a very important lesson being taught in these verses. The lesson is that it was not that Elisha was upset at these boys for making fun of him, but it was the principle that his position was worthy of honor. Elisha understood that it was not he who was worthy of honor, for he was simply a mere sinner, but the position that he held was worthy of honor. It was because of this that he called the she bears to destroy these young men.

Every person needs to realize the importance of their position and the position of the man of God. I believe that we should learn to address the preacher properly, not because he is something, but because his position is something. As I write this book, the President of our country is President George W. Bush. Now when you address the President, you would never address him as "President George," for that would be disrespectful to the position that he holds. When we address the President we always address him as "President Bush" or "President George Bush" because this is giving proper respect to his position. Likewise, the preacher's position is worthy of respect. I believe we should learn to address the preacher properly, not because he is something, but because the position he holds is something. If I was the pastor of a church, I don't believe people should address me as "Bro. Allen" or "Pastor Allen." This would be disrespectful to the position that I hold. I believe that if I was the pastor of a church that the people who I pastor should address me as "Pastor Domelle" or "Bro. Domelle." We have lost respect for position in America, and even in the world. We have let this casual mentality sweep through our nation and it is destroying the honor of the position of the man of God. I believe that whenever you address someone you should address them properly, not because they are someone, but because the position that they hold is worthy of respect and honor. We must be careful to hold the positions of people in high esteem and address them properly, especially the position of the man of God.

14. He let God's power speak for him.

As we close the chapter you will notice in **2 Kings 2:14-15** that Elisha did not have to tell people that God's power was upon him, the works that God did through him spoke for themselves.

If you get the power of God upon you, trust me, you will not have to publicize how much power from God you have. The works that follow you will say it for you. We need not worry about telling others how much of God's power we have upon us. Instead, we need to simply do the works of God with His power and let those works speak for themselves. I am not saying that preachers should not tell of how God has filled them with His power, for I think this is important, but the best voice for God's power on your life are the works that God has done through you.

Looking at the life of Elisha we can see that he did get that double portion upon his life and he did pick up the mantle of the man of God. As a second-generation Christian, he realized he should do more than the previous generation, and he did. I hope and pray that every second-generation Christian who reads this book will determine to pick up the mantle of the previous generation and go and do twice as much as the generation before you. Don't be satisfied with average. We should be above the average and we should do more than the generations that preceded us because we have learned from them. We should carry on from where they left off so we can go to new heights for God.

13

God's Trophy Piece

Job 1:8, "And the LORD said unto Satan, Hast thou considered my servant Job, that there is none like him in the earth, a perfect and an upright man, one that feareth God, and escheweth evil?"

Job 1:22, "In all this Job sinned not, nor charged God foolishly."

When you think of trials and enduring trials the way a Christian should endure them, nobody shows us how to endure trials in the proper way like Job does. Job is the epitome of how to endure trials. When you see someone who is going through several trials in their life, many times we will say about that person, "They are a modern-day Job." What hardships this man faced! Yet in all the hardships that he faced he never accused God in a foolish way. He never lost his integrity throughout the whole ordeal. What a Christian Job was! God believed in Job so much that He challenged Satan about the goodness of Job. You see, Job was the trophy piece that gave God bragging rights to Satan regarding one of His servants and how good he was. God could do this because He knew Job, even though he was still human and had weaknesses that he needed to improve on, he could be trusted to face and endure trials in the proper way. Let me tell you the story so that you can see why Job became a trophy piece for God.

Job was a very wealthy and well-known man in his day. On top of these qualities, Job was also a very godly man. As you read the story of Job, you will see he was a man that daily sacrificed to God and daily made sure that he kept his heart clean from sin. One day Satan came to appear before God to accuse the people of God, and God said to Satan, **"...Hast thou considered my servant Job..."** Satan responded to God that the only reason why Job was such a good man was because God had placed a hedge about him so that Satan could not touch him. Therefore, God gave Satan permission to afflict him, and that Satan did. In one day, as Job was sitting in his house, a servant came to Job and told him that his oxen had been stolen by the Sabeans and his servants were killed. Oxen are a symbol of work in the Bible, so in all reality Job had just lost his job. As this servant finished speaking, another servant came in and told Job that his sheep and servants had been burned up by the fire of God. The sheep was a way to measure wealth in those days, so this was the equivalent of losing all of his money. When this servant finished speaking, another servant came in to inform Job that his camels had been stolen by the Chaldeans. A camel was their form of transportation. When this servant finished speaking another servant came in and told Job that all of his children were in a house together when the roof caved in, and they were killed. What tragedy this man had come upon him in such a short time. He had, in just a few minutes, lost his job, wealth, transportation, and children and yet he did not charge God foolishly with his mouth.

Satan again appeared before God on another day, and God again bragged on Job. Satan asked God to give him permission to touch the body of Job, to which God gave this permission, only Satan was not to take Job's life. The Bible says that after all of these tragedies, Satan then afflicted Job with painful boils from the top of his head to the bottom of his feet. Now Job had lost his health. Then, as he sat in the ashes of what he had left, his wife came to him and encourages him to just curse God so that he could die. Now his wife has forsaken him. To top it all off, his so-called best friends came and began to criticize him when what they should have done was help him. Here Job lost his friends. Think with me: he lost his job, wealth, transportation, children, health, wife and friends and still did not accuse God in a

185

foolish way. In all this he never lost his integrity or his Christianity. No wonder he was a trophy piece for God.

How all of us need to learn to be like Job when trials come our way so that we can fill God's trophy case with trophies. Let me show you some of Job's characteristics so we can copy them and become one of God's trophies.

1. He avoided evil at all cost.

As you read in **Job 1:1** and **Job 1:8**, you will notice that God mentions twice that Job was a man who eschewed, or escheweth, evil. The word "eschew" means "to avoid." In other words, Job was a man who avoided evil. Now as we have learned previously in this book, evil is not just sin, but it is doing sin with the intent to hurt someone. When God said that Job was a man who eschewed evil, God was saying that Job was a man who avoided trying to hurt other people. Job was the type of man who would go the extra mile to be sure that he treated others right.

How important this is to understand! If we are going to become a trophy for God, we must be like Job and do everything in our power to avoid hurting other people. Now I am not saying we should compromise in order to accomplish this. What I am saying is that we need to go the extra mile and, if needs be, go well out of our way to be sure that we avoid hurting other people.

The best way I have found to do this is to live by ethics. God's people need to learn to live by ethics. When you live by ethics, then you will do what is right at all costs. The ethics that we hold ourselves accountable to may not be followed by others, but they need to be followed by us. We cannot always expect others to live by our ethics. We should not be concerned with whether others are living by our ethics, but we should be concerned about ourselves living by our own ethics. You need to be sure that you do everything in your power to treat people right. Listen, you can stand for right and still treat people right. You don't have to run over people in order to do right. How important it is for the world to see God's people not just living right, but also treating others right while they do what is right. Let me ask you a question: do you do everything in your power to be sure that you treat people the right way? Do you make sure that whatever you do to others you would not mind it if they did the same to you? This is truthfully what ethics are. Ethics is simply living and treating others the way you would desire for them to treat you. How important this attribute is, for this is how our Saviour lived and this is also how Job lived. Most certainly, this is how you should live if you want to become a trophy piece for God.

2. He was not too rich for God.

In **Job 1:3**, God tells us of the wealth of Job and all that he possessed. Job was a very wealthy man in his day. Though Job was wealthy, he still served God and did right. Why? Because Job was not too rich for God. Job did not let his money become his god; instead he became the god to his money. Job would not let his money dictate how he was going to live his life. He realized that his money was simply a tool that he could use to serve God.

Money should never be an issue between you and God. When money becomes an issue between us and God then money becomes wrong. When we are more concerned with making money than we are with serving God, then money has become our god. God is not impressed with how much wealth we have. We should realize that the money we have was loaned to us by God anyway. Do you think that God is impressed with the millions, or even the billions of dollars that a person may have in their bank account when God owns the whole world and everything inside of this world? Do you really think that God is impressed with our money? We need to realize that we should never become too rich for God. It matters not how much money you have, you are to still serve God, go to church and win souls every week.

187

I think of my good friend Dr. Russell Anderson. Dr. Anderson, so far in his lifetime, has given over thirty-five million dollars to the work of the Lord. As he and I have preached around the country together, I have heard him say several times that there was no business deal that ever kept him out of church on Sunday or Wednesday night. Neither did his money stop him from being a soul winner for God. I have seen very few men in my lifetime who witness for God as much as Dr. Anderson does. I have personally watched him lead several people to Christ. He has never become too rich for God. He could take the monies that he has earned in life and use them all for himself and his family, or he could use those same monies to try to impress society, but instead he has used his monies, the monies that God has given him, to finance the ministries of the Lord. He has used his money to start eleven Bible colleges around the world. He has used his money to help start over eight hundred churches. He has also used his money to finance Christians overseas to be full-time soul winners. He has realized that God did not give him this money for his own use but for the use of God's work. As a layman in a church, he could have used his money and become too rich for God. Instead, Dr. Anderson has taken the money that God gave him and has given it back to the work of the Lord.

Let us never, no matter what is offered to us, become too rich for God. Let us realize that the monies God has given to us are simply loaned to us to help us do His work while we are here on this earth.

3. He was not a lazy person.

Now I am not going to spend much time on this, but I believe I needed to mention this quality about Job. I believe that this quality was one of the reasons why Job was a trophy piece for God. It says in **Job 1:5** about Job that he "**...rose up early in the morning...**" Job was not a lazy person.

God will never put a lazy person in His trophy case. God uses people who are hard workers and are not lazy. God Himself is not a lazy God, in that we see He worked six days just to make this great world in which we live. We need to learn to be workers and to work even when we don't feel like working. If we only work when we feel like it, then we will not work most of our life.

4. He led his family spiritually.

Look again at **Job 1:5** and read what it says, **"And it was so, when the days of their feasting were gone about, that Job sent and sanctified them, and rose up early in the morning, and offered burnt offerings according to the number of them all: for Job said, It may be that my sons have sinned, and cursed God in their hearts. Thus did Job continually."** Now you will notice about Job in this verse that he was a spiritual man. Not only was he spiritual, but he led his family in being spiritual. He did not tell them to serve God as he sat at home. No, Job served God by example. His family had an example to follow in serving God.

Every home needs this if the home is going to be a godly home. I believe that the man should be the leader of the home spiritually. I know that we live in a politically-correct society that tries to downplay the man's leadership role in the home, but God's Word is still the final authority. God's Word still says that the man is to be the leader in the home. This does not mean that the woman or the children are just a bunch of idiots and are sub-humans who must be servants to the man. What the Bible teaches us is that someone has to answer to God for the home and God has chosen the man to be the one who answers to Him for how the home is run. This is why the man is to be the leader in the home. Every man should be the leader in the home when it comes to spiritual matters. He should not force them to do something that he is not doing. Instead the man should lead in the home by example by doing what he expects his family to do. I believe the man ought to read more Bible than anyone else in the

189

home. I believe he ought to pray more and win souls more and be more spiritual than anyone else in the home. Not because he is better than they, but because he is the leader. It is high time that the men of our day step up to their leadership roles and start leading in their homes and in their churches and lead them down a Biblical path.

As I touch on this subject, let me say to the family, as the man leads in the home then the family should follow as he leads. Don't make the man have to pull you along spiritually. Ladies, don't make your husband have to pull you along spiritually because you just don't want to get involved in the church. Children and teenagers, don't make mom and dad have to pull you to church and pull you to serve God. Instead, the home should be a dad leading in the home with wife and children hand-in-hand following him as they all follow Christ. This is what God intended when He set up the home.

5. He was not one of the crowd; he was his crowd.

Look at **Job 1:8**, and you will notice when Satan came to appear before God that God did not have a lot of people on whom He could brag. All God had to brag on at this time was Job. Now Job was not the only person alive during this day. There were probably several thousands of people alive, and yet God only had one person to brag on. Why was this? Because Job was not a man who ran with the crowd; he was a man who was his own crowd. He was not spiritual because everybody else was being spiritual; he was spiritual because he chose to be spiritual in spite of the society of his day.

Yes, if you are going to be a trophy piece for God then you will have to learn to be spiritual even if the crowd is not spiritual. As you look at the average Christian of this day you will find most people will only do what the crowd is doing. What a shame that we have such weak Christians in our day. God uses people and brags on people who learn to stand alone. Look at most of the characters in the Bible whom God used in a great way, and most of them were people who had to stand alone. Christian, are you only spiritual when everybody else is spiritual? Does your spirituality depend upon the spirituality of the crowd? How this society needs a good dose of Christians who are spiritual, not because it is popular, but because it is right. You look at the average Christian today and the average Christian only follows the crowd and what the crowd will do. I have seen several young people who, when they go to the Christian school, are spiritual young people, but once they graduate they backslide and become just like the world. Why is this? Because they are depending upon the spiritual temperature of the crowd to determine their own spirituality. Even preachers of our day need to learn that if needs be, stand up and do what is right even if all the other preachers are not doing right. I watch preachers of today who are wondering which way the winds are blowing in their movement to decide what they are going to do. What a shame! Preachers should do what the Bible says in spite of what the majority of preachers are doing. You will never become a trophy piece for God by being one of the crowd. You only become a trophy piece for God by doing what is right in spite of the crowd.

6. He had a right perspective concerning trials.

We come to the part of Job's life for which he is known, and I believe we should study how he endured the trials that he faced. As you look in **Job 1:21**, you will see that Job had the right perspective concerning the trials that came his way. He realized God had given Him everything that he had and that God also had the right to take away from him what He had given to him. He realized God did not owe him anything. God did not owe him any possessions and God also did not owe him any explanations. In fact, as you come to the end of this verse you will see that Job said, **"...and the LORD hath taken away; blessed be the name of the LORD."** When you can say this, then you have the right perspective concerning the trials in your life.

191

Your perspective of the trials that you face only shows your perspective of God. You show me how you face trials, and I will show you what you think about God. Listen, the only hope of coming through trials the proper way is to keep your trials in their proper perspective. You must realize that God does not owe you anything. When you start demanding that God owes it to you to treat you better, then you are only setting yourself up to become bitter towards God. We need to understand that God has a right to give us bad as well as good. If God has the right to give us good in life, then mind telling me why He does not also have the right to allow the bad in our lives? You must realize that God does not allow the bad because He is trying to hurt you. God allows the bad for your good and for His good. God only has your best interest in mind, and God knows that if we are ever going to become better people and be used in a greater fashion by Him, He must send trials our way to purify us. It is only through the trials of life that we are purified. Christian, if the truth be known, if you were to weigh the good that God has given to you against the bad, you would find out that the good far outweighs the bad. Until you start having the proper perspective concerning trials, you will never become one of God's trophy pieces.

7. He realized that God was good to him all the time.

In **Job 1:21-22**, you will see Job realized that God was good to him when times were good and that God was also good to him when times were bad. Job never one time accused God of not being good to him.

I don't know what you are facing in your life as you read this book, but may I say to you that no matter what you are going through, God is still good to you. God is not good just when we think He is good, but God is good to us all the time. It is always easy to say that God is good when you are on the mountain top of life, but tell me that He is good when you are in the valley. I have learned in my life that when the valley comes I need to tell God that I still believe that He is a good God. How every Christian needs to stamp the thought in their mind that no matter what they face in life, God is still good. God's goodness is not just good in the good times but God's goodness is good all the time, including when times are bad for us. His goodness is not determined by the conditions that we are facing in life, but His goodness has been determined before there ever was a world, and His goodness never fails. As **Psalms 52:1** says, **"...the goodness of God endureth continually."** Yes, God is good to us all the time!

8. He did not always say what he thought.

Look at **Job 2:10**, as Job speaks he says, **"...What? shall we receive good at the hand of God, and shall we not receive evil? In all this did not Job sin with his lips."** This was said to his wife after she encourages him to curse God so that God would kill him. Now to be quite honest, Job probably felt like telling God what he was thinking in his heart, but Job was wise and never one time let the thoughts that he was thinking come through his lips.

When you are going through the trials of life you must learn to keep a bridle on your tongue. How careful we should be in charging God foolishly when we are hurting. You may have thoughts of wanting to approach God and tell Him what you think, but I believe we should be very careful about what we let come out of our lips when we are facing trials. We should remember that God has feelings, too. If we were created in His image and He created us with feelings, then this would mean that God has feelings, also. Now I know that God does not carry His feelings on His shoulders like we humans do, but I would not want to say something that could hurt the feelings of God. I would not want to say something that would hurt His feelings because He thought higher of me than I do of Him. All of us should be careful about saying something to God in a time of hurt that we would regret later on when the hurt is gone. This is why we must be careful about saying everything that we think, for sometimes our thoughts, if worded, will be regretted later on. Sometimes we need to learn to keep our

193

mouth shut and not say anything at all, realizing that God is good to us no matter what we may be facing.

9. He was a helper to the hurting.

When you read **Job 4:3** you will see that Job spent his life helping those who were going through many of the same heartaches that he was now facing. Now the very things he had helped others with had come to him. How commendable this is about Job. He was a man who spent his life helping those who were going through tough times in life.

Many of us should become like Job in this area of helping those who are hurting in life. I can promise you that there is no greater ministry a person can have than to help those who have hurting hearts. Yes, God likes it when we help those who are hurting. Who better to become a trophy piece for God than those who help the hearts of the hurting as Jesus did in His life. But let me remind you, when you are going through the same trials of life that you have helped others with, the counsel that you gave to them is just as good for you as it was for them. Sometimes in our trials we need to go back to what we have told others to do when facing the same trial. This counsel and advice that we gave to others is not of less value because we are going through trials. If it was good for them then it will be good for us.

10. He lived an open life spiritually.

In **Job 6:10** Job says, **"...I have not concealed the words of the Holy One."** What was he saying when he said these words? He was simply trying to get the point across that when he lived his life for God he did not live it in a concealed manner; he lived it openly so everyone could see it.

This is the type of Christian we need today. We need the type of Christian who when they go to the job they do not conceal their Christianity, but they let everyone on the job know they are a Christian. We ought to be open about the life that we live for God. Jesus did not come in a concealed manner to this earth and hide that He was the Son of God. No, Jesus came and proclaimed openly to those with whom He came in contact that He was the Son of God. We in like manner should copy the example of our Saviour and not be ashamed to let others know we are Christians. When it is time to eat at the restaurant, don't be ashamed to bow your head and thank God for the food. When in the schoolhouse and running with your friends, don't be ashamed to let them know that you cannot do certain things because you are a Christian. No matter where we go and no matter whose presence we are in, we should always proclaim Whom we serve and not be ashamed of being a Christian. Christians need to learn to live their lives openly as Christians without shame.

11. He did not put God on trial.

Job 13:15 says, **"Though he slay me, yet will I trust in him: but I will maintain mine own ways before him."** Job, though going through the toughest time of his life, told God that there was nothing He could do to get him to stop serving God. Job told God that even if He decided to take his life, he would still trust Him and serve Him because his service to God was not on trial. Job did not try to threaten God that he would stop serving Him if God was not good to him. Instead, Job told God that his service to Him was unconditional.

Christian, stop putting God on trial and stop telling God that if things don't get better then you will stop serving Him. Our service to God should never be on trial with God. How many times have we seen people try to bargain their service to Him if He will just make things better for them? Oh, I wish that Christians would grow up and just serve God because it is right to serve God. We should never put God on trial! What we should do is what Job did and that is tell God that even if He decides to slay us, He is going to be stuck with us no matter what! Now this is true Christianity! The type of Christianity that will serve God when He is good to us and then will stop serving God when we don't think He is good to

195

us is so shallow. Every Christian needs to, at some time in their life, determine to prove to God that they will serve Him even if they lose everything in life. You see, it is always easy to serve God when times are good. You show me the one, though, when times get bad who still says that God is good, they still read their Bible, pray, go soul winning and attend every church service, and I will show you a true Christian. When God sees that we love Him no matter what He may allow to come our way, then God knows that He has someone whom He can make into a trophy.

12. He never lost hope in a time of hopelessness.

How was it that Job never lost hope though his life seemed to be a wreck? We find the answer in **Job 19:25-27**. Job said he kept his hope by looking to the other side of life. He knew if these trials were to take his life, that his Redeemer was still alive and that he would see Him if he died. That is how he kept his hope alive in times when it seemed like there was no hope.

Christian, you always have hope even when it may seem like there is no hope. Our hope is that one day we will go to a place called Heaven. If the only hope we have is Heaven, then we have a great hope. It is in this place called Heaven that all heartaches and sorrows and pain will be gone. If in life it seems like you have no hope, then may I advise you to just look to the other side and realize that if all else fails in this life, our Redeemer still lives and Heaven is still our home. Our sins are gone if we are saved, and that place called Heaven will be our home when this life of sorrow eventually passes away. What a hope we have! A hope that one day we will go to Heaven and see, with our own eyes, our Redeemer, Jesus Christ. This is how you keep hope in times of hopelessness.

13. His integrity was not for sale.

I probably like this part about Job more than anything else. He says in **Job 27:5**, "**...till I die I will not remove mine**

integrity from me." Job was informing us that though he may have lost everything in life, he was not going to lose his integrity or character. He realized that sickness may take his health but it could not touch his integrity. He realized that banks may take his homes and his cars but they could not take his integrity. He realized that life may take his children from him, but it could not take his integrity from him. He realized that family and friends may leave him and he may be left all alone, but one thing he could never lose was God, and one thing they could never take from him was his integrity. He said that if the only thing he had left in his life was his integrity, then he was not going to lose that.

The test of your character is how much character you still have when you have lost everything in life. Character only becomes character when times get tough, for this is what defines your character. You should never put a price tag on your character. Your character is the one thing this world cannot take from you, and you should hold strong to your character no matter what you lose in life. You only have one name and if you let the hard times take your character also, then you will have nothing at all.

As you read about the life of Job, certainly at the end of the book you will see that he never lost his integrity. He realized the value of integrity and said that he would hold onto that no matter what the cost may be. Christian, hold onto your integrity and never put a price tag on it, for it is only in tough times that you can prove the purity of your character.

14. He prayed for those who tried to hurt him.

I don't know if anything in this entire story speaks to the greatness of Job more than this point here. In **Job 42:10** we read, **"And the LORD turned the captivity of Job, when he prayed for his friends: also the LORD gave Job twice as much as he had before."** This takes a good Christian to do what Job did here in praying for his friends after they had attacked him and slandered him and his character. Yet Job had the character and Christianity to pray for them, I believe, in a good way. What did he pray about? Well if you look earlier in the passage you will see that God was very angry with Job's friends and I believe that maybe Job prayed that God would be merciful to them. I believe when God saw that Job was willing to pray for his friends that God would be merciful to them, it was then that God decided Job had enough of the hard times that he was going through.

When you can pray honestly for God to bless your enemies or even those who have been spiteful towards you, then you have become what God wants you to become: like Jesus. This is what Jesus did when He was on the cross, and this is most certainly one of the qualities of a mature and great Christian. I ask you, how much do you pray for those who have been spiteful towards you? If you do pray for them, then are you praying that God would be good to them and bless them? This is the sign of a person whom practices true Christianity and this is the type of person who God would want to use as a trophy to brag about. This type of person mirrors what Jesus is like.

In closing, let me say about the life of Job, these are just some of the characteristics of his life. This is certainly not all of his characteristics. I do believe you have seen what made up the character of Job and the reasons why God used him as bragging rights to Satan. Would to God that those who read this book would become more like Job so that God, when Satan comes to accuse the brethren, could find more people He can brag about to Satan. Why not try to give God a reason to brag about you and make you one of His trophies?

Products Available from Allen Domelle Ministries

Preaching CD Albums

- Caution, Hot Preaching Ahead
- Sermons for Struggling Christians
- Relationships with God and Man
- Sermons for Hurting Hearts
- Miscellaneous Sermons – Volumes 1 – 5

Books

- How to Study the World's Greatest Book

To Order These Products call
(304) 839-9532
or visit
www.domelleministries.com.